TOURISM IN MALAYSIA

TOURISM IN MALAYSIA:

AN EMPIRICAL STUDY ON SOCIO- ECONOMIC AND ENVIRONMENTAL IMPACTS

AUTHORS:
A.H.M.ZEHADUL KARIM
HAZIZAN MD. NOON
NOOR AZLAN MOHD NOOR
NURAZZURA MOHAMAD DIAH
SOHELA MUSTARI

PARTRIDGE

ISBN:	Softcover	978-1-4828-7996-4
	eBook	978-1-4828-7995-7

Print information available on the last page.

To order additional copies of this book, contact
Toll Free 800 101 2657 (Singapore)
Toll Free 1 800 81 7340 (Malaysia)
orders.singapore@partridgepublishing.com

www.partridgepublishing.com/singapore

Contents

Acknowledgement And The Prologue

Being strategically located at the gateway of global routes with an impressive eco-environmental setting, Malaysia attracts a huge number of tourists and visitors every year from abroad who arrive in this country most frequently with modest expectations and aspirations. For that reason, tourism has been identified as one of the largest service-oriented industry in Malaysia, contributing to at least 10% of the country's GDP and providing employment to millions of people. In this context, if we consider tourism positively it can be said to be a good source of income, creating job opportunities for a huge number of local people and positioning them as economically competent individuals in the community. Nevertheless, tourism may also cause a negative effect in which the local culture may be assimilated into the alien norms and behaviours through a continuous process of acculturation. It is also learned that due to day-to-day interactions with the tourists and visitors, there occurs tremendous socio-cultural impact on local values which contextually requires to be redefined. Furthermore, from the ecological perspective, tourism accelerates expansion of the urban settlement causing damages to the natural eco-system by replacing the natural habitats with pavement and unprecedented urban settlement. From this perspective, this research is designed to examine people's perceptions and feelings about the socio-cultural and environmental impacts of tourism in Malaysia by conducting an empirical research in Klang Valley, adjoining Kuala Lumpur city.

This book is the outcome of a concerted research effort which has been conducted on tourism in Klang Valley, Malaysia, between 2012-2014 to proliferate its empirical viewpoints in regard to the impacts of tourism in the community. As a product of group research, this volume owes much to its co-researchers and colleagues in the Department of Sociology and Anthropology at the International Islamic University Malaysia (IIUM) who have remained committed to this research in all phases. I owe a great debt to these colleagues of mine and other faculty and staff members who have been supportive in various ways to complete this empirical research and finally get it published in the form of a book.

If we carefully look at the shelves in the library, it is distinctively clear that there has been numerous books and literatures which have been published on tourism since the beginning of the 1960s. Most of these remarkable books and literatures on tourism (e g., Theobold, 1994; Tisdel, 2004) are compiled as edited volumes providing us with valuable theoretical basis and framework on the subject, but many of these however, do not consider focusing on the empirical aspects of tourism. While there is general consensus that many of these books on tourism contain very valuable articles, there is no denying the fact that the empirical aspect of the issues remains fully ignored. Although there has been a valuable addition by Tisdel who in fact, compiled a number of articles, of which many have emphasized on tourism from the empiricist viewpoint, most of them however, have not elaborated their discussion from a holistic perspective. As a matter of fact, being inspired by Tisdell and a few of his collaborative researchers, we venture to write this book on tourism in the Malaysian context. With the paucity of empirical investigation, this book is an introduction to assess the views of community people in the Klang Valley areas of Kuala Lumpur in Malaysia.

One article from this research was presented at an international conference in Tokyo (IUAES 2014) and another has been published in South Asian Anthropologist (Serials Publications) in 2014. These two brief articles were later elaborated and expanded to be included as part of chapters in this book. It must be admitted here that in no way are these the same writings; rather, they are expanded, modified and rewritten for inclusion into this book. Apart from this, we have also given proper references of those writings so as to make it clear and evidential. The article published in the South Asian Anthropologist (see Karim *et al.,* 2014) also received an IRRIE award in 2015 for its credibility and recognition of merit from International Islamic University Malaysia for which we are grateful to the Research Management Centre (RMC) of IIUM and the university itself.

When people move from one place to another with a desire to get some recreation, this movement then may be regarded as part of tourism[1]. Malaysia is rich with natural resources which attract many tourists to come and visit its beauty. Being strategically located at the gateway of global routes with an impressive eco-environmental setting, Malaysia attracts a huge number of tourists and visitors from abroad who arrive in this country most frequently with certain expectations and aspirations. For that reason, tourism has been identified as one of the largest service-oriented industries in Malaysia, contributing to at least 10% of the country's GDP and providing employment to millions of people. There was about 16.43 million tourists arrived in Malaysia by the year 2005, adding an amount of 32 billion ringgit in the national coffer, principally through foreign earning which sharply increased to 65.44 billion in 2013 with the increase of 25.72 billion foreign tourists viasiting the country (see Table 1, p-10). In this context, if we consider tourism positively, it can be said to be a good source of income, creating job opportunities for a huge number of locals and positioning them as economically competent individuals in the community. Nevertheless, tourism may also cause a negative effect in which the local culture may be influenced and the alien norms and behaviours assimilated into it through a continuous process of acculturation., Russel (2003), for that reason, aptly mentioned that tourists may come and go but their presence may have some permanent impact of it which might bring some irreparable loss to the nation from socio-cultural and environmental points of views. It is also learned that due to day-to-day interactions with tourists and visitors, there occurs tremendous socio-cultural impact on local values which contextually requires to be redefined. Furthermore, from the ecological perspective, tourism accelerates expansion of the urban settlement causing damages to the natural eco-system by replacing the natural habitats with pavement and unprecedented urban settlement. From this perspective, this research is designed to examine people's perceptions and feelings about the socio-cultural and environmental impacts of tourism in Malaysia through an empirical investigation of Klang Valley, adjoining Kuala Lumpur City.

Dr. A.H.M.Zehadul Karim

Chapter 1

Introductory Background

Malaysia is perhaps one of the most unique countries of the world, which is strategically situated at the gate-way of a number of countries passing through its international sea routes with a wonderful eco-environmental setting. Being a pluralistic society, it inherited its own traditional culture with harmonious integration of the diverse ethnic groups living in a very peaceful and politically stable situation. Due to such eloquent features, people from abroad become largely attracted to this land and thus they frequently arrive here as visitors and tourists. As recently as in 2005, it is reported that at least 16.7 million international tourists from outside had visited Malaysia bringing until then about 30 billion ringgit in terms of foreign currency into the country (see Badruddin *etal.*, 2006). It is evident from the table that this number has been increasing very consistently every year and finally in 2013, the total arrival of the tourists in Malaysia stood at 25.72 million importing 65.44 billion ringgit as foreign currency (see Table 1 for details). For that reason, it is quite likely that tourism industry, with a target towards economic expansion, has been moving rapidly in Malaysia.

Accordingly, this research assesses the prospect of tourism in Malaysia as part of Southeast Asia, and thus shows the relevance of this issue in the wider global context. From that point of view, the research is designed to show the importance of tourism in this country and accordingly it conceptualizes a theoretical paradigm for future research on tourism in Malaysia. Based on that thematic viewpoint, the book has thus three important issues which are discussed in different sections. First, it makes a review of the relevant literatures and makes an annotation of those literatures to justify the suitability of them in regard to Malaysian tourism. Secondly, the book also highlights the scope of tourism in Malaysia by identifying various issues related to it. Based on that discussion, the paper finally conceptualizes an appropriate paradigmatic model suitable as guideline for conducting our own future research and other future studies on tourism in Malaysia. Finally, based on our discussion, the work also explores the scope of tourism in Malaysia and also locates the prospects of it in Malaysian context.

Malaysia: Its Regional Setting and Multicultural Features as Tourist Spot

Malaysia is located at the center-point of SouthEast Asia, comprising a federation of 13 states and three federal administrative territories. Peninsular Malaysia covers some 132,000 square kilometers of land being separated from Sabah and Sarawak which together comprises 60% of the total land area of Malaysia and are separated from the Peninsular Malaysia by a distance of 500 kilometers across the South China Sea. Sabah constitutes an area of 74,000 square kilometers and Sarawak has another 124,000, square kilometers of land collectively known as East Malaysia (see Leete 2007). Sabah and Sarawak have wonderful eco-environment, full of naturalbeauty inhabited by multicultural groups of people including the Christians and a few *orang asli* (indigenous) communities. East Malaysia is situated to the north of the island of Borneo bordering Brunei Darussalam and an Indonesian province named Kalimantan (see Leete 2007 for details).

At present, tourism may be regarded as the largest service-oriented industry in Malaysia contributing at least 10% of the national GDP and it is expected that it will provide employment to 100,000 million people, which certainly seems to be very positive in this respect. As a requirement, it obviously becomes essential to build infrastructural development, new accommodations and also make improvements on the available hotels and catering services. Simultaneously, it will have to facilitate better transportation and communication to make it more comfortable and enjoyable for visitors from the eco-environmental perspective. The overall physical development with infrastructural improvements of roads and highways thus will allow visitors easy access to their desired destinations and provide them better expectations. Such developments may eventually benefit the local inhabitants who are living in those areas permanently. From the sociological point of view, it is also useful to preserve the architectural heritage; and accordingly, reconstruction and renovation of architectural buildings and monuments of historically significant places are required. From that perspective, if we consider tourism positively, it can be said that it is a good source of income, creating job opportunities for a huge number of people Malaysia. In addition, business investments of various types related to tourism such as opening many markets, shopping-towns, hotels and restaurants can also take place.

Based on such worldview and conceptualization, we go further into identifying a few important issues on Malaysian tourism. From the economic point of view, Malaysia has been regarded as an emerging nation having the potential to increase its annual GDP and showing a considerable improvement every year. It has been included as one of the five tigers of Southeast Asian region, having glorious success in terms of economic and infrastructural developments. Tourism in Malaysia has also been regarded as a good source of its economic earnings; in that context, it has a special significance. Until now, there has not been any sort of demographic pressure nor has it have any shortage of land resources. Upholding its carrying capacity, Malaysia should not allow ruthless and abrupt destruction of its natural resources in the name of tourism. As a matter of fact, tourists from abroad often come to this land to seek the natural beauty and also to observe its culture and heritage. For that reason, we would say that instead of modernizing tourism, Malaysia should emphasize more on ecotourism. This is economically sustainable and simultaneously it allows the nation to protect the environment and its ecology.

A few writers (e g., Mohamed *et al.*, 2006) have given special importance to island tourism in Malaysia and we believe that due to some special geographical advantage, the country should proceed into popularizing ecotourism, linking it to the countryside. In fact, it may be advantageous as it generates good income for the people living in the coastal areas and eventually it may be a good strategy to reduce poverty among the surrounding islanders. In this context, Hall's (2007) edited book titled "Pro-poor tourism: Who Benefits" which compiles a number of articles focusing on how tourism should be directed towards economic benefits for poor residents is worth mentioning here. The book adds that the most important target of tourism and the direct benefit of it should be designed for them.

Due to rapid economic development and infrastructural improvement in Southeast Asian, a huge number of tourism markets have expanded in this region especially centering on Singapore, Thailand, the Philippines and few others. Tourism in Thailand and Singapore has become quite attractive as people from the western world feel comfortable in adjusting to these regions due to easy interactions with the locals. From the religious and cultural points of view, the situation in Malaysia is fully different from their neigbhouring countries. Furthermore, both nations have been able to preserve their historical heritage and architectural monuments o in the city centers (see Karim 2010).

Apart from infrastructural development and business facilitation, tourism has also other socio-cultural benefits in this regard. It brings civic pride and social prestige for Malaysia by making international linkages in the global context. It takes Malaysian culture abroad and people from outside can get in touch with unique Muslim heritage in the Malaysian context, among others.

It must not however be thought that tourism always has some adverse effect on the environment. To make the environment attractive and natural, conservationists often emphasize on ecological preservation. The most important negative aspect of tourism in Malaysia is that it may often have some impacts on the traditional cultures and values of the local people. It is said that many local people often want to imitate foreign culture, wearing western attire and leaving behind their traditional way of living. In some areas, people suspect the presence of some socially-prohibited and illegal activities which may have some negative impacts on the society and culture in general (INSAN, 1989).

Map 1

Malaysian Map showing some Important Geo-Administrative Locations

https://www.cia.gov/library/publications/the-world-factbook/geos/my.html

Table 1: Arrival of Tourists in Malaysia with a total Earning Assessment (1998-2013)

Year	Arrival of Total Tourists	Total Revenue (in Ringgit)*
1998	5.56 Million	8.60 Billion
1999	7.93 Million	12.30 Billion
2000	10.22 Million	17.30 Billion
2001	12.78 Million	24.20 Billion
2002	13.29 Million	25.80 Billion
2003	10.58 Million	21.30 Billion
2004	15.70 Million	29.70 Billion
2005	16.43 Million	32.00 Billion
2006	17.55 Million	36.30 Billion
2007	20.97 Million	46.10 Billion
2008	22.05 Million	49.60 Billion
2009	23.65 Million	53.40 Billion
2010	24.58 Million	56.50 Billion
2011	24.71 Million	58.30 Billion
2012	25.03 Million	60.60 Billion
2013	25.72 Million	65.44 Billion

Source: Rearranged and Modified from Experience Malaysia, Tourism Malaysia 2014. *One dollar equals to approximately 3 ringgit or a little more at present time.

Apart from this, there are innumerable ecological effects and environmental impacts. Due to tremendous infrastructural development, there have been massive constructions of buildings, the opening of new shops and super-markets, additional roads and highways, all of which eventually and make a totally transform the traditional settlement. Due to rapid over-urbanization, many crises and urban-related social problems emerge in the surrounding areas at the community level, creating social nuisance.

From the ecological perspective, the expansion of urban settlement causes damages to the natural eco-environment as natural habitats have been replaced by pavements, buildings and urban settlement. The loss of trees and green space due to deforestation affects the flora and fauna as lands are replaced by urban settlement including hotels and restaurants. These are undoubtedly negative consequences impacting directly on the environment.

Because of these positive and negative aspects, we must assess the carrying capacity that a particular society may allow for optimal tourism. In this context, we will assess the Klang Valley areas to understand their present situation, to see how far these areas are able to support Malaysian tourism. This information will be procured from the administrative record-keeping documents of different government and non-government sources responsible for designing tourism in Malaysia.

We have already given an indication in our previous discussion that, like many other Southeast Asian countries, Malaysia has similar prospects for tourism. While the major activities of tourism are based on international visitors coming to this country, the main components of tourist expenditure and economic interaction have great influence on Malaysian economy. Detailed information as to how tourism benefits the local people from the commercial perspective has been gathered. At the same time, the research will make an estimation of the GDP contribution of tourism in regard to Malaysia's economic welfare. It is learned that due to day-to-day interactions with tourists and visitors, there occurs a tremendous socio-cultural impacts on local values and social structures which contextually require to be redefined. From that perspective, the research is designed to identify the socio-cultural impacts of tourism on traditional Malay culture. More specifically, the research ascertains local people's perception on tourism, whether the local people are accepting tourism from socio-cultural and religious points of view or are treating it as a threat to Malaysian communities. At the same time, the research generates a comparative line of data to know the differences in perceptions between the professionals and the local community about the impact of tourism on their socio-cultural and environmental lives. The research will assess the positive aspect of tourism by locating socio-cultural status that Malaysia derives from internationalism at the global level. It will take Malaysian heritage to the global level and the international community will be able to see how diverse groups of people live in a harmonious co-existence.

The research also focuses on the negative effects of tourism particularly natural, man-made and socio-cultural environments. The negative effects can be seen in the unwelcomed socio-cultural effects, increased vandalism, and loss of the normative and ideological Muslim heritage. It is well recognized that tourism in Malaysia often damages the eco-environment of Klang Valley which is said to be over-used by the tourists. The natural habitat is destroyed due to over development of the roads, highways, buildings and shopping centres. The demand for new space results in deforestation and loss of agricultural and vacant land which eventually is responsible for an increase in air pollution and greenhouse effect. The expansions of urban and peri-urban areas are also responsible for the displacement and depletion of wild varieties of rare animals.

Chapter 2

Study Area, Methodology And Data Sources

This research on tourism is based on first-hand empirical data collected through field research; at the same time, the research relies on secondary information gathered through reviewing different literature, reports and articles at the national and international levels. The research relates to an approved project on tourism which was undertaken in Klang Valley[1], Kuala Lumpur[2], Malaysia for more than two years between 2012 to 2014. The areas which were covered in this research included the whole urban and peri-urban localities in Klang Valley locations of Kuala Lumpur and Selangor.

Klang is the oldest Royal Town of the State of Selangor and it is one of the main gateways to enter Malaysia through sea. Klang Valley, from which we collected extensive data, is geographically located in the north and south zones of it, marking Klang River on both sides of it. Both these zones are clearly separated from each other by the river. Because of some administrative importance Klang South becomes quite busy during the weekdays and in the weekends, the area simply turns into a center for social and recreational activities, especially after office hours and on holidays. It may be noted here that the biggest port of Malaysia named Port Klang is also located at Klang South. The etymology of Klang further suggests that its nomenclature has been taken from Klang River that runs through the town itself. The entire geographical area thus is surrounded by the river which begins in Kuala Lumpur and runs westward all the way to Port Klang. The whole region is now known as Klang Valley where Kuala Lumpur City is located and this study is based on Klang Valley, focusing most intensively on its surrounding areas located within Kuala Lumpur.

Kuala Lumpur is the capital city of Malaysia and is located in Klang Valley[2]; it comprises 1.4 million people of whom, 45.9% are the Malays, 43.2% are the Chinese, 10.3% are the Indians and the remaining 0.6% are of different ethnic categories. Circumscribed by the Titiwangsa Mountains in the east, and Sumatra island of Indonesia on the west, Kuala Lumpur belongs to a tropical rainforest climatic zone (see Map in Wikipedia 2012).

This final product of this research has been guided by an exploratory study based on empirical data collected in the field. It generates socio-anthropological and first-hand information of the primary sources at the micro-level investigation. The research covers multiple aspects of field studies seeking views from a cross-section of people. The principal investigator and two other research assistants have employed participatory approach to make it more meaningful. Among various other steps, the research formulates an interview with a few professional persons from a cross-section of people. This enabled us to know their opinions in regard to socio-cultural and environmental impacts of tourism.

To make an in-depth exploration at the field-level, the research generates a questionnaire to interview all the heads of families living in that region with a target of making a total enumeration of two closely located central urban neighbourhoods in Klang Valley. The two study sites[3], Taman Impian Ehsan and Taman Midah in the Klang region were chosen because of their near location to Ampang and its neighbouring areas which are regarded as well-frequented tourist areas. Both Taman Impian Ehsan and Taman Midah are easily accessible from the main city centers and the local people living in these areas always interact with tourists in their everyday life as most of the tourists usually stay in the hotels located near these places.

This type of quantitative data allowed us to generate survey-based information about various aspects of tourism in the Malaysian context. Apart from these interviews, the research has additionally conducted two FGDs (Focus Group Discussions), utilising one with the local people at the community level and the other one with foreigners who have come to Malaysia temporarily. This provides us with instant data relating to tourism. The FGDs are conducted by the principal investigator himself along with his doctoral student as facilitator who was directly involved with the research.

More specifically, we have some additional information about Klang Valley and its surrounding regions by making an assessment of the areas in regard to then capability to bear the load as a tourist spot in terms of its carrying capacity. This allows us to know as to how far Klang areas will be able to support Malaysian tourism. We have procured all these information from the administrative record-keeping of different government and non-government sources designed for tourism in Malaysia. It may be noted here that one doctoral student with her profound knowledge and background on environmental sociology has worked as key-investigator, supervising data collection at the field level. Along with the principal investigator/author of this research, she also collected some important data in this regard. The reason for using several methods based on triangulation in this research is simply to gain confidence and reliability in terms of its methodological strength. A brief outline of the research methods is shown below in a tabular-form to earmark each specific activity.

Table 1: A Tabular Description of Different Aspects of Data Collection Procedures

Data Gathering Activities	Tools of Data Collection	Number of Respondents or Size of Sample
Household Survey of Two Urban communities in Klang Valley Areas	An all-inclusive structured Questionnaire	(Locality 1: N=100+Locality 2: N=100) = Total Number of Respondents: N=200
Interview with Tourists	Based on Structured Questionnaire	A total of 150 tourists and visitors coming to Klang Valley Region from different parts of the world.
Sample interview with Professionals	Based on a pre-designed checklist	2 Professionals having expertise on environment.
In-depth interviews	Based on a pre-designed checklist	10 interviewees in total
FGDs	Based on target-focusing checklist	2 FGDs seeking views from national and international respondents regarding the impact of tourism in Malaysia.

Chapter 3

Conceptualizing Tourism: Theoretical Framework And Review Of Literature

Conceptualizing and Describing Tourism:

Based on Webster's Dictionary, the term 'tourist'[4] designates a person seeking a journey from his own place to another where he returns to the starting point; making a kind of circular trip which may be targeted for business, pleasure, relaxation or education. This definition combining recreation and business has not been accepted by many with the argument to denounce it having some professionalism as part of it. Accordingly, Mieczkowski (1981) refutes the etymological meaning by Webster by saying that most tourism is recreational in nature, for which business, professional and service-related personal or group tours may not be included. Recreation, according to Mieczkowski (1981), entirely falls within the purview of leisure situation involving free or discretionary time leading to 'revitalization' or relaxation of the mind and body. To endorse Mieczkowski's view in a different perspective, Murphy (2013) adds that "part of this recreational activity takes place outside *his* local community and as a result travel becomes an important component" (p.9). In this context, travel and movement is an important way "to discover the unknown, to explore new and strange places, to seek changes in environment and to undergo new experiences" (Robinson 1976: XXI). Although Mathieson and Wall's (1982) definition seems to be very simple, the sense clarifies that, "tourism is the temporary movement of people to destinations outside their normal places of work and residence, the activities undertaken during their stay in those destinations, and the facilities created to cater to their needs" (p.1). Thus, tourism has been conceptualized as a temporary movement of the people towards outward destinations having resided there usually for a shorter period of time with embodied experiences (see Mathieson & Wall 1982; Bucckart & Medlik, 1974). "Basically, tourism is a movement in space from a person's home district to one or more destinations and then back again" (Aronsson, 2004: 23-24). It denotes a short term movement of a person from one particular settlement or region where he stays permanently as home-based settlement to an outside place which is absolutely different from his present one. In providing a conceptual framework of tourism, Alistair Mathieson and Geoffrey Wall (1989: 14) outline three basic elements of tourism: firstly, it involves the stay in some selected destinations; secondly, as part of it, the tourists are concerned with effects on the economic, physical and social sub-systems with which they are interacting more or less very closely during the time of their visitation in a foreign land. Thus, tourism has been identified as a composite phenomenon incorporating the diversity of interactions and relationships which are found in the tourists' travel process (see Mathieson & Wall, 1989 for details).

There are enormous literatures (e.g. Mason, 2010) saying that prior to the 1960s tourism was not very popular as traveling at that time was quite expensive. At the same time, traveling in those days was not very comfortable either in terms of communication and safety. But the situation has changed gradually in the last few decades and since the 1960s, tourism has become more fulfilling for people who are adventurous. Now, it has turned into a global phenomenon with further expansion of ICT and the development of telecommunication system. Air routes have also been expanded. Initially tourism was only limited to certain countries of Europe and North America but now it has expanded to Asia and other continents.

Tourism is a recent economic force in global trade and presently it is often been regarded as an 'industry' specially involving varieties of people sharing their socio-cultural activities and economic transactions through personal interactions. It is estimated that tourism provides direct and indirect employment to at least 200 million people and it was forecasted that tourism related jobs throughout the world would generate 350 million available works by the year 2005 (see Smith, 1995). There are a few literatures (e.g., Lea, 1988; Smith & Eadington, 1992; Hall & Brown, 2006; Hall, 2007) which have exemplified the economic development of tourism in some developing nations of the world through the extensive use of tourism and the utilization of its potential role for humans' well-being, a topic which has also been well documented in those writings. Despite having such importance, research on tourism has just started and as such, the number of empirical researches is still few.

Yet, there are a few important literatures which provide us with the right direction in expanding our academic horizon in regards to the 'epistemology of tourism', relating the fields of environment and social science (e.g., Hohl & Tisdel, 1995; Bryden, 1973). Among the literatures available in the field of tourism, we will cite valuable discussions in the next few paraghraph. These will help us to conceptualize our proposed research in the field of tourism in relation to the Malaysian context. At the very onset, we may begin with the issue of tourism discussing it mostly from a theoretical viewpoint.

Smith (1995) has written a book on tourism which includes a total of 11 chapters covering all aspects of its demand-side. as an emerging industry. In this book, geographical aspects of tourism have been specially focused through descriptive and partial statistical interpretations. At the very beginning of the book, it provides us with an overview of research on tourism and thus has given us with all the theoretical definitions based on historical update.

Muller and Jansson (2007) edited a book entitled "Tourism in Peripheries: Perspectives from the Far North and South". A total of 14 papers from diversified disciplines focusing on the contributions of a number of scholars from different countries have been incorporated in the proceedings which were earlier presented in a conference on tourism. Taking regionalism as the main focus of interest, the papers highlight tourism from the perspective of space, place and environment and the presenters mostly correlate the issue of tourism with regional development. One of the papers, "Organizing Tourism Development in Peripheral Areas: The Case of Subarctic Project in Northern Sweden" was written by Malin Zillinger (2007). It indicatively focuses on tourism in the sub-arctic network in Northern Sweden to attract foreign tourists in the region, providing a possible economic gain for the people of that locality (see Zillinger, 2007 for details).

Chart 1

An Annotation of Some Significantly Relevant Books and Articles Relating to Tourism Research in Global and National Contexts

Name of Author(s) and Title of Book	Principal Theme and Main Contents of the Study
Adrian Franklin (2003) Tourism: An Introduction	This book is designed to provide a guideline in understanding the theory, practice and development effects of tourism in general. It considers general theories of tourism and as such deals with tourism as social and cultural phenomena. The book is sequentially divided into three parts, each one of them is designed to be self-standing and can be understood into and conceived as a critical evaluation of tourism.
Stephen L.J. Smith (1995) Tourism Analysis	This is an introductory book offering immense discussion on asking, knowing and answering basic questions relating to tourism. With discussions on a variety of quantitative methods drawn from numerous sources in the social sciences, the book presents them in clear step-by-step style.
Peter E. Murphy (2013) Tourism: A Community Approach	The seminal work of Peter Murphy offers a comprehensive examination of tourism development by taking a community approach which allows for a balanced assessment of tourism in the industrial nations of North America and Western Europe. The book advocates the adoption of an ecological approach to tourism planning which will permeate tourism with general community goals and planning strategies.
Rhonda Phillips and Sherma Roberts (2013) (Eds). Tourism, Planning, and Community Development	The introspection of tourism and community development is a fascinating issue which has been depicted in this book with an inclusion of nine articles intricately connecting tourism planning with community development. From the diverse perspectives, the book discusses the complexities of tourism planning which can be daunting to communities as they revitalize the existing efforts on tourism.

Telfer and Sharpley (2007). Tourism and Development in Developing World	This book explores the nature of tourism development by investigating the challenges and opportunities which developing countries have been facing.
David A. Fennell (2008) Ecotourism	Fennell's book on Ecotourism poses a view saying that there are enormous literatures on tourism which in fact, do not cover the eco-tourism perspective. It comes as no surprise to attempt begin this study by giving explanations about mass and alternative tourism, relating them to sustainability and carrying capacity. In fact, the book is useful for the discussion on social and ecological impacts of ecotourism.
D.K.Müller & B. Jansson (2007) Tourism in peripheries: Perspectives from the far North and South	Access to peripheries is an important strategy to develop and popularize tourism. This book reviews the scope of tourism development by involving the peripheral zones as part of the discussion where a total of 14 papers from diversified disciplines treat regionalism as the main focus of interest.
Clem Tisdell (2001) *Tourism Economics, the Environment and Development: Analysis and Policy*	A total of 27 articles have been included in this book where Tisdel's sole contribution is quite prominent. Most of the articles except for a few are authored orco-authored by Clem Tisdel. The content of the book has four parts covering various dimensions of tourism development.
Bella Bird (1989) *Langkawi--from Mahsuri to Mahathir: Tourism for Whom?*	The Institute of Social Analysis INSAN published this book specifically to focus on Langkawi, an island in Malaysia. The book raises some important issues relating to tourism in Malaysia particularly about some drawbacks of destroying resources which have social impacts and cross-cultural influence.

C. Michael Hall (Ed.) (2007). *Pro-poor tourism: who benefits? Perspectives on Tourism and Poverty Reduction* (Vol. 3).	Hall's book deals with tourism as part of reducing poverty among the local people. Using tourism as a tool for economic development has been an important direction for many developing nations.
Richards & Wilson (Eds.). (2007) *Tourism, Creativity and Development*	This book shows th relationship between tourism, culture creativity and development supported by ongoing empirical research in many different countries of the world.
Rhonda Phillips & Sherma Roberts (Eds.). (2013) *Tourism Planning, and Community Development*	Community development and tourism planning are fascinating discursive at the present time. The complexities of tourism planning and community development can be daunting challenges to revitalize tourism.
Mohamed, Som, Puad, Jusoh, & Kong (2006) Island Tourism In Malaysia: The Not So Good News	The study indicates that although tourists are bringing in lots money providing income for the people and the government there have been some unforeseen impacts of tourism where the localities are losing their natural beauty and originality.
Hall & Richards (Eds.). (2002) *Tourism and Sustainable Community Development.*	Tourism and community development has been the main theme of this book which identifies tourism as a primary resource. A total of 20 articles focusing on diversified aspects of community were incorporated to relate them to tourism.
Mathieson & Wall (1982) *Tourism, Economic, Physical and Social Impacts*	The unprecedented expansion of tourism has given rise to increasingly pronounced economic, physical and social impacts. This book highlights as to how these impacts affect the society and culture.
Ti Teow Chuan (ed.). (1994) Issues and Challenges in Developing Nature Tourism in Sabah	As part of nature-tourism, this book is a compilation of a number of articles presented at an international seminar organized in Sabah, Malaysia which mostly focus on ecotourism in Sabahas an important spot.

Nor' Ain Othman (2007). Tourism Alliances and Networking in Malaysia	This book is an overview of tourism industry in Malaysia that focuses on its growth, performances and income generating trend by providing the situation with selected markets. The book makes some important comments in line withtourism in Malaysia and some recommendations.
INSAN (1989). Langkawi—From Mahsuri to Mahathir: Tourism for Whom?	The book is a documentation on staying and observing the island Langkawi for a few months. The book has highlighted the contradictions by drawing the viewpoints of the people for whom tourism has caused negative effects that do not properly benefit the local people residing on in the island. They are trapped in poverty after being too much involved in tourism and leaving their agriculture.

(Source: Updated, Rewritten, Expanded and Modified from Karim et al., 2014).

One of the articles written by Lovelock (2007) presents data on visitors' perspectives on 'Naturalness and their Consequences in New Zealand' which has brought useful information relating to the attitudes of tourists. This aspect of seeking opinions from the tourists about preserving the natural habitat seems to be quite relevant for our research. In our proposed study, we may also seek suggestions and views of the local people in regard to preserving the natural eco-environmental habitat without destroying them at large. We may also seek suggestions of foreign tourists to make the tourists' centres attractive to them.

Pro-poor tourism as a perspective of reducing the poverty of the local people has been highlighted in a book edited by C. Michael Hall (2007). By employing tourism as a tool of economic improvement of developing countries, the book includes a number of articles (e g., DeKadt, 1979; Lea, 1988; Smith & Eadington, 1992) that focus on particular aspect. In this context, Hall's contribution is academically very significant and crucial as the book includes a few papers which discuss tourism in different regional settings.

Ashild Kolas (2008) has published a book entitled "Tourism and Tibetan Culture in Transition" explaining a processual and historical reconstruction of the Tibetan culture which was found to be commercially beneficial and economically suitable. From the spatial point of view, the stakeholders of tourism have targeted constructing and reframing Shangrila for promoting tourism in that region. There is much to learn from tourism in Shangrila as to how a particular place gets contested for reinvention.

The importance of tourism has been highlighted in a very useful compilation by Clem Tisdell (2001), a Professor of Economics from the University of Queensland where the author has incorporated a wide range of documentation showing tourism as highly dependent on environmental conservation. The book is particularly suitable as a total of 27 articles in this compilation reflect observatory writings on different ecological settings. In this volume, Clem Tisdel and David L. Mckee (1988) have written a paper entitled "Tourism as an industry for the economic expansion of archipelagoes and small island states" identifying tourism as a tempting force to decentralize population. Based on their assumption, it may clearly be hypothesized that the marginally poor people from highly densed areas of a nation could often be diverted to tourist spots to utilize their petty businesses for subsistence.

One of the articles written by Rajasundaram Sathiendra Kumar and Clem Tisdel (2001) focuses tourism as the principal force as well as an important source of economic development for Maldives in the Asia-Pacific region. In that research, it was found that the economic development based on tourists' points of view seem to be quite significant for our proposed study where we may seek suggestions and views of a few outsiders, enabling us to make future plans. Furthermore, the paper seeks the opinions of the local people, asking for their suggestions in regard to the preservation of their eco-environment, without destroying the natural habitat. The inner thrust of this study allows us to accept eco-tourism as an alternative strategy which minimizes the destruction of natural resources and instead, encourages the preservation of them.

In the Southeast Asian context, during the early part of the 1990s, an international conference on tourism was held in Kuala Lumpur under the sponsorship of the Department of Urban and Regional Planning of University Technology Malaysia to examine the tourism contexts of this region. Among a number of contributors, Badri Bin Haji Masri (1991) has provided us with a valuable documentation on the growth and prospects of domestic tourism in the Southeast Asian region. Another paper presenter named Yeo Nai Meng (1991) in the same conference highlighted the trends and prospects of tourism in the 1990s in Singapore and Malaysia, identifying Asia Pacific region as the fastest growing tourist region of the world.

A more relevant research has been conducted by Mohamed *et al.* (2006) which specifically mentions the significance of tourism in the Malaysian economy. The paper discusses tourism development on a few islands of Malaysia, namely, Langkawi, Pangkor, Tioman and Redang, providing us with valuable information on the impact of tourism in the development context. The research assesses both positive and negative impacts of tourism on these islands which have been pressurized tremendously, overlooking the carrying capacity of these areas. Based on such directions, this proposed research is intended to focus on Klang Valley as a study region to identify all aspects of socio-cultural and environmental impacts of tourism in Malaysia.

Chapter 4

Tourists And Visitors In Malaysia: Trends In Arrival And Their Socio-Demographic Parameters

Trends in Tourists' Arrival

In assessing local people's perception of tourism in Malaysia, it seems to be quite logical to visualize the trends in tourists' arrival and at the same time, have an idea about the types of people who are making trips into this country. Contextually, we provide here a background profile of the visitors coming to Malaysia and produce a sense of reconciliation to bring them together for a socio-cultural and economic interaction. In view of this consideration, a total of 150 tourists from 23 different countries including 25 Malaysians from other regions were identified and interviewed; have been found to be visiting Klang Valley and its surrounding places in Kuala Lumpur. It is reflected from our data that apart from visitors coming from a number Asian countries, visitors also came from West Europe, the Middle-East, Australia, Canada and the United States. While talking to these visitors very informally during the interviews, it can been ascertained that the tourists are exceedingly happy and satisfied with the treatment they receive from the local people. Most of the respondents regard Malaysia as climatically and geographically suitable and ethno-politically a peaceful country.

It was learnt from the visitors that the majority of have come to Malaysia to fill their leisure time for vacation but there are also a few visitors who have come for business and education while, the remaining are visiting their relatives and friends who are staying in Malaysia. The most fascinating tourist activities are sightseeing and visiting the shopping malls and enjoying food in different hotels and restaurants. Many visitors are attracted to the hills and beaches. Others are fond of walking, hiking, trekking, scuba diving/snorkeling and participating and enjoying diversified cultural events in Malaysia (Nor' Ain Othman, 2007).

Socio-Demographic Characteristics of the Tourists

Tourists' socio-demographic information and profile statistics is reflective of their social background which is particularly useful and notably relevant for policy planners of host countries. Accordingly, it provides some basic data on those tourists who are travelling to Malaysia as temporary visitors. Tourists in Malaysia belong to different ages, being both male and female (M=62%, F=48%). Younger people below the age of 35 years (45.3%) and middle-aged persons coming from the age category of '36 to 50 years' with a 33.3% are found to be quite dominant in the ratio as tourists to Malaysia. Nevertheless, the older tourists above 50 years of age however, are not lagging for behind as they are also responding very positively having a content of 20% of the visitors. Although 39% of the visitors are Muslims coming from the neighbouring countries of SoutheEast Asia, South Asia and the Middle East, the Christians constitute 25% of the visitors followed by the Hindus consisting 20%. The remaining 6% of the visitors come from other diversified religious groups composing Buddhists, Sikhs and others. This is indicative that from the socio-cultural point of view, Malaysia is a preferred tourist-spot for diverse ethnic and religious groups of people from all around the world. Although China, Vietnam and Myanmar are close neighbours of Malaysia, very few people from those countries come to Malaysia, the reason however, is unknown to us.

With regard to the educational background, it is discernible that tourists by nature remain well-educated and qualified; this hypothesis has proven to be true in our research when all the tourists in our study sample are found to be educated. Among the 150 visitors, 103 (72%) are graduates, diploma-holders and/or have received college education while the remaining 28% have completed their post-graduate studies. Visitors in Malaysia are multi-professionals where government servants represent 17% of the visitors. Among the other tourists, private service-holders constitute 28%, business personnel comprise 25%, students remain 17% and the retirees represent 16% of the sample.

Apart from age and education, affluence and global knowledge often influence attitudes towards having motivations for a tourist. It is quite likely that "individuals with low disposable incomes are less likely to pursue travel arrangements which involve (first class) air-fares, expensive hotels and costly restaurants, than those who are wealthier" (Mathieson & Wall, 1989: 29). Thus there is a positive connection between socio-economic variables and the tendency towards recreation and travel. In regard to behavioural characteristics of the tourists, Allister Mathieson and Geoffrey Wall (1989) in their writing identify a few indicators like motivations, attitudes, needs and values of tourists as crucial for making a move towards outside. They have aptly correlated these variables with tourists' socio-economic profiles for which the visitors become motivated in going on tours (for details see Mathieson & Wall, 1989: 29).

Visitors' choice of Places as tourists in Malaysia

Reports on tourists' choice of places in Malaysia can be delineated through their flow of visitation of different spots and locations in the country. It is discernible from Table 2 that tourists coming from abroad invariably have to make a stop-over in Kuala Lumpur as it is the first entry point of most tourists entering this country through air-route. Initially, tourists' arrival in Kuala Lumpur provides them with a spectacular developmental impact of the city with its global orientation. It gives the visitor an impression of having an intermingling of the East and the West.

The city itself provides good facilities of modern and comfortable hotels and restaurants with well-connected transportation facilities to get access directly to the inner-side of the city centers. As learned through our informal interviews, tourists instantly become attracted by the facilities provided by Kuala Lumpur International Airport (KLIA) which is located in Sepang, some 60 kilometer from the city abounded with 10,000 hectares of land. KLIA has an excellent express train service, which takes the passengers into the main city enclave in less than half an hour. There are also limousine taxi services controlled by the airport authority allowing travelers to reach their destination with reasonable fares and security. These obvious receptions of the tourists encourage them with a comfortable stay-over in Kuala Lumpur since they are arriving after a long-distant travelling from abroad. This has been evident when all 150 visitors clearly mentioned that they are extremely happy to visit Malaysia in general and Kuala Lumpur in particular, as tourists.

We have pointed out earlier that the visitors feel quite strongly being in Malaysia as tourists because of their special liking of different things as outlined below in the following discussions. But with regard to their specific choice of places, we asked them to indicate which places in Malaysia they have already visited. It is apparent from Table 2 that almost all the respondents admitted that they have already taken a run through Kuala Lumpur, moving around the Klang Valley areas of the city. Besides Kuala Lumpur, a great majority of the tourists have visited Pahang (60.67%), Malacca (76.67%), Penang (60%) and Langkawi (60%). It seems that these few places are very much favored by the tourists due to their unique geo-physical and environmental locations. Apart from these important places, a good number of tourists have also visited Johor (37.33%), Kelantan (19.33%), Terengganu (12.67%), Ipoh (12.33%) and Perlis (10.67%). Since Sabah and Sarawak are located on the other part of western Malaysia and are quite far across the sea, many tourists are reluctant to take another air trip to these states. Yet a few of the tourists have already visited Sabah (4.67%) and Sarawak (4.67%), being attracted to their wonderful natural environment and divergence of cultures. Due to the presence of a number of indigenous groups of people in the states, a few tourists are attracted to Sabah and Sarawak.

Table 1: Tourist and Visitors by Their Country of Origin*

Country of Origin	Number of Visitors (N=150)	%
Algeria	4	2.6
Australia	19	12.7
Bangladesh	6	4
Canada	4	2.6
Egypt	9	6
Finland	6	4
Germany	3	2
India	7	4.7
Italy	4	2.6
Malaysia	37	24.7
Nigeria	6	4
Pakistan	6	4
Palestine	3	2
Russia	2	1.3
Saudi Arabia	3	2
Singapore	2	1.3
Somalia	3	2
Syria	5	3.3
Thailand	3	2
The Netherlands	4	2.6
U.S.A	2	1.3
UK	5	3.3
Yemen	7	4.7
Total	**150**	**100**

*Based on a sample survey of 150 tourists as found on the basis of their availability.

Tourists' Most Attractive Places of Choice

On the basis of their personal choice of places, the tourists were asked to mention three important places in Malaysia which they like as visitors in this country. It is evident from our data that a great number of them have given their choices of Malacca (9.33%), Pahang (14%), Penang (18.66%)), and Langkawi (12.66%). It is evident from the table that most visitors choose these places as their second and third choices (see Table 3 for details). In regard to Kuala Lumpur, at least 42 (28%) tourists favoured the city as their main place of liking. It seems that as a tourist spot, Kuala Lumpur has all its privileges and infrastructural facilities which invariably attract the visitors from outside.

Table 2: How many places in Malaysia did you visit so far? (N=150)

Places Visited	Frequency	Percent
Kuala Lumpur	150	100
Pahang	91	60.67
Malacca	115	76.67
Penang	90	60
Ipoh	19	12.67
Johor	56	37.33
Langkawi	90	60
Kelantan	29	19.33
Sabah	7	4.67
Sarawak	7	4.67
Perlis	16	10.67
Terengganu	19	12.67

Table 3: Tourists' Most Attractive Places in Malaysia

	Placed as 1st Choice (N=150)		Placed as 2nd Choice (N=150)		Placed as 3rd Choice (N=150)	
	f	%	f	%	f	%
Kuala Lumpur	42	28	34	22.66	25	16.66
Pahang	21	14	19	12.66	23	15.33
Malacca	14	9.33	17	11.33	16	10.66
Penang	28	18.66	20	13.33	26	17.33
Ipoh	7	4.66	0	0	12	8
Johor	12	8	19	12.66	16	10.66
Langkawi	19	12.66	22	14.66	27	18
Other places	7	4.66	19	12.66	5	3.33

Some special attributes usually remain important to the tourists in choosing a particular place for visit and in this regard, Malaysia has some unique features for which tourists from home and abroad become fascinated to visit. Two of the essential elements of tourism everywhere in the world are infrastructural development and transportation facilities as tourists by nature always want to reach their destination very comfortably without facing any hassle or hazards. Contextually, it must be admitted that Malaysia has excellent transportation facilities throughout the country with enormous well-built roads, highways and railway linkages. Its North-South Highway connects Singapore and Thailand passing through a number of big cities and towns; the Karak Highway links the west coast region with that of eastern coast of Malaysia. Singapore and Thailand are also well-connected to Malaysia by railway services where trains are plying frequently everyday. Malaysian Airlines (MAS) and a few other airlines provide domestic services to almost all the major cities and towns of the country and at the same time, these airlines connect East Malaysia with West Malaysia through regular air services day and night. MAS and many other international airlines have regular connections to Singapore and Thailand making Malaysia attractive and convenient to the tourists. Since Malaysia is located between Singapore and Thailand, international tourists visiting these countries more often get attracted to come to Malaysia as it is near to these countries and moreover, it is a peaceful and progressive Muslim nation. Although Thailand and Singapore have many colourful features which provide stiff competition for Malaysian tourism it is no denying that its soberness and modesty certainly encourage tourists to go on family trips to this country to enjoy its diversified cultures with homogenous living.

What actually attracts tourists Malaysia was a question posed to the visitors. Diversified factors make Malaysia popular to them and among these, the most significant is, its multiculturalism and ethnic integrity. Most of the respondents opined that they like the co-existence between the Malays, Chinese and Indians making Malaysia very popular to the people in other countries. They also find it very clean and well organized.

Table 4
Reasons why the Visitors like Malaysia as a tourist spot

1. A very peaceful country
2. Well organized and Clean
3. Beautiful weather and frequent Rains
4. Natural beauty, hills and greenish environment
5. Melancholy beaches
6. Multicultural Society
7. Lucrative infrastructural development
8. Nice place and friendly people
9. Malaysia has both Asian and Western flavours
10. Unique traditional culture with diversified food

Apart from this, the natural beauties of Malaysia with its hills and wonderful greenish environment are simply God-gifted features as the country receives sufficient rainfall in moderate weather. Malaysia is also famous for its eco-environment with many islands and beaches providing the visitors with sight-seeing and an enjoyable melancholic atmosphere. Island tourism in Malaysia has been assessed by Badruddin Mohammad et al. in 2006 who identified four prominent islands of Malaysia namely, Langkawi, Pangkor, Tioman and Redang and thus evaluated the real and perceived physical impacts of tourism on these Malaysian islands. Based on their assessment, it may be predicted that if these islands are maintained properly by protecting their natural and eco-environment, there is every possibility that these islands will attract foreign visitors looking for scenic alternatives. But at this time, due to tremendous pressure of local and foreign visitors, these islands are surpassing their carrying capacity an thus losing their original beauty. Badruddin et al., (2007) maintain that "The influx of mass tourism has indeed opened the islands to all, making them defenseless against the negative impact brought by the tourists" (p.1219). Badruddin et al. (2007) however, should not be blamed for such caution as they are rightly concerned about the calculative damage to the islands in Malaysia. To make it more accurate, we therefore suggest for very modest and well-thought policies where both natural protection of the islands and their carrying capacity could be taken into consideration to optimize its use through popularizing ecotourism.

Table 5
Visitors' Special attraction for Klang Valley* as a Tourist Spot

1. Multicultural region with ethnic diversity
2. Natural view
3. Diversity in food and culture
4. Weather and rains
5. Twin Towers and Putrajaya City
6. Historical monuments
7. Rapid transport and communication system
8. Attractive mega shopping malls
9. Asian and Western flavors
10. Genting Highlands of Klang Valley and a few important attractive sights

*Klang Valley is simultaneously identified as Kuala Lumpur.

The visitors take into consideration a number of features that make Klang Valley attractive and the right place to visit. This view is fostered by the visitors mentioning the factors which according to them are most important reasons for choosing Klang Valley in general and Kuala Lumpur in particular, as a tourist spot in Malaysia. If someone visits Klang Valley, it is justifiably observable that the tourists' assessment regarding Klang Valley is quite proper as the area is truly a mixture of many local and foreign nationals resulting in multiculturalism. It is also essential mentioning here that having enormous development, Kuala Lumpur has an excellent eco-geographic beauty which is circumscribed by seas with natural hills and mountains.

It has attractive mega shopping malls surrounding the Twin Towers and Putrajaya City. Kuala Lumpur also provides diversity in food and culture where tourists always get a mixed flavor of Asian and western cuisine. The whole city is supported by low-cost rapid transport (LRT) having stations in all central places; it also has other train and bus services connecting all suburban areas of the city, easing transport and communication systems.

Chapter 5

Local People's Perception Of Tourism In Malaysia

Chapter Five is the documentation of a survey conducted on 200 families from two centrally located peri-urban communities which are mostly inhabited by local Malaysia's. As mentioned earlier, these two peri-urban communities are Taman Impian Ehsan, situated near to UPM (University Putra Malaysia) and Taman Midah located close to Ampang, a very busy commercial zone of Kuala Lumpur. Both these communities belong to broader Klang Valley region within the circumscription of Kuala Lumpur.

The main purpose of this survey is to know the attitudes of the local people in regard to tourism in Malaysia. The respondents of the survey are from three major ethnic groups of local residents (i.e., Malays, Chinese and Indians) living in the areas which shows a clear domination of the Malays representing 85% of the families interviewed in this research. Since the Malays are overwhelmingly Muslims, their religious affiliation also indicates that they are the adherents of Islam.

All 200 respondents in the survey are found educated and many of them (at least 71%) are also well conversant in English which allows them to interact with the tourists very comfortably.

Table 6
Socio-demographic Characteristics of the Respondents from Two Household Surveys: STUDY AREA: KLANG VALLEY

Demographic Traits and Characteristics	TAMAN IMPIAN EHSAN (UPM) N=100	TAMAN MIDAH (AMPANG) N=100
Age (In years)		
Up to 35 (Young)	58 (58%)	52 (52%)
36-50 (Middle-aged)	31 (31%)	30 (30%)
51 & above (Old)	11 (11%)	18 (18%)
Sex		
Male	51 (51%)	47 (47%)
Female	49(49%)	53(53%)
Religion		
Muslim	85 (85%)	91 (91%)
Hindus	7 (7%)	2 (2%)
Christian	5 (5%)	2 (2%)
Buddhists	3 (3%)	5 (5%)
Language Spoken		
Malay	85 (85%)	89 (89%)
Chinese	7 (7%)	7 (7%)
Indian	8 (8%)	4 (4%)
Education		
Up to SPM	58 (58%)	44 (44%)
Diploma	24 (24%)	30 (30%)
Bachelor	13 (13%)	16 (16%)
Master's degree & above	5 (5%)	10 (10%)

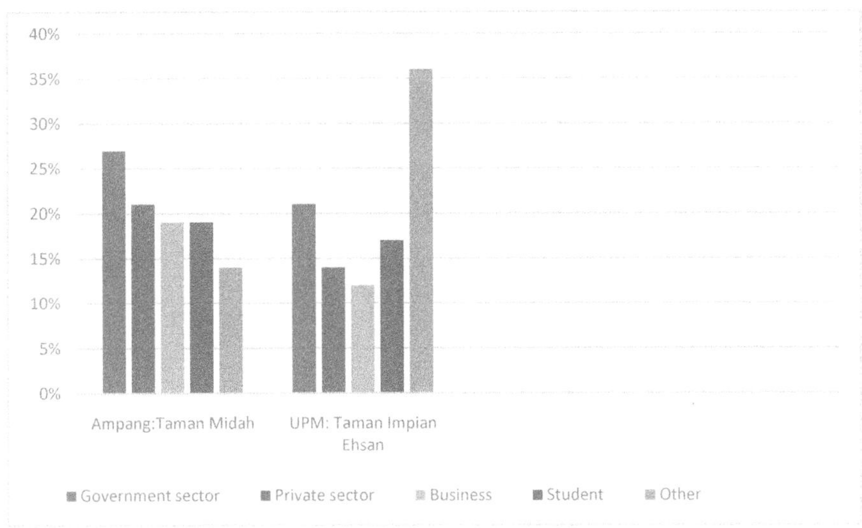

While asking the respondents about their impression of the tourists from outside visiting Malaysia, as many as 92% of the residents admitted that they are well aware of their arrival into this country. As a matter of fact, they are not fully unhappy about the latter's visit to Malaysia; rather, they have good liking for them as many of the residents in the Klang Valley find it as good opportune to earn some extra money from this source. The local people staying in these communities have high regard for Klang Valley as a tourist spot as it has plenty of attractive places which may impress the visitors. But simultaneously, they are also concerned and worried about the cultural dissimilarities which often hurt the sentiments of the local people for which many of the respondents (58 -59%) expressed their dissatisfaction, saying that tourism affects many aspects of their culture.

Table 7: Attitudinal Views of the Community Regarding Tourism

	COMMUNITY 1: TAMAN IMPIAN EHSAN	COMMUNITY 2: TAMAN MIDAH
(a)We are quite aware of the tourists visiting Malaysia. We never knew that the tourists are coming to this country.	94 (94%) 6 (6%)	90 (90%) 10 (10%)
(b) Yes, I like tourists visiting our country. No, I do not like visitors coming to this country.	90 (90%) 10 (10%)	84 (84%) 16 (16%)
(c) I think that the local people can increase their income due to the arrival of tourists to the country. No, local people's earning is not at all dependent on tourists and visitors.	63 (%) 37 (%)	53 (53%) 47 (47%)
(d) Yes, Klang Valley is a very suitable place for tourism. No, Klang valley does not seem to be a suitable place for tourism.	89 (89%) 11 (11%)	77 (77%) 23 (23%)
(e) Many cultural issues get affected due to tourism. No, I do not find any cultural problem in having tourism.	58 (58%) 42 (42%)	59 (59%) 41 (41%)

It has been mentioned earlier that Malaysians in general, do not pose much negative attitude to the foreign visitors and this has been proven when we find that 87% of the respondents from the two communities of Taman Impian Ehsan and Taman Midah mentioned that they like tourists visiting their country (see Table 7). With a view to identify the reasons for which they like tourists visiting their country, a series of responses emerged. These are: (a) increase in economic transactions (b) Malaysia becomes known to other persons; (c) people can learn foreign languages and get acquainted with their cultures and (d) it is proven that Malaysia is the right and conducive place to visit and so on (see Table 8 for details).

Notwithstanding the positive responses, a few respondents felt that tourism has many negative effects on their communities, such as: (a) it affects national security and (b) tourists often create unnecessary pressure on the Malaysian population by contributing enormously to the degradation of the environment. They further suspect that the foreign tourists often get involved in drug trafficking and there is also a possibility that local people often become exposed to the HIV/AIDS. These issues often remain questionable as exposure to HIV/AIDS might be very unlikely and drug trafficking is not that frequent as airport authorities remain cautious about them. Residents of local neighborhoods often face some unaccustomed behavior which often annoy them to some extent; yet many people however do not take it very seriously as they believe and show tolerance in the name of internationalism and multiculturalism.

Table 8: Whether the Respondents like visitors coming to Malaysia from other countries

Based on Positive Responses received from 184 persons from Two selected Communities	Based on Negative responses received from 16 persons from Two selected Communities
• Economic transaction increases. • We can learn foreign languages and also get acquainted with their cultures. • Malaysia becomes known to other persons from abroad which is a pride for us. • Increases local income. • It is proven that Malaysia is the right and conducive place to visit. • The visitors can get to know Malaysian culture. • Economy boosts through tourism • Keeping good relationship with other countries.	• It affects national security. • Tourists create unnecessary pressure on our population which contributes to the degradation of the environment. • Often there remains the possibility of drug trafficking and also the local people might be exposed to hidden HIV/AIDS. • Unaccustomed behaviour of the tourists.

The community people have ideas about the good and bad elements of tourism. When asked to identify the good elements, most of them mentioned that it increases the flow of economy and simultaneously enhances job opportunities for the local people. Then there are other views saying that the local people get exposure to other cultures and also they have a feeling that the arrival of more tourists into the country indicates that Malaysia gets introduced to many nations of the world. In regard to its utility, the community people also think that it allows the people to acquire foreign languages which makes them proficient in English as they have to communicate with the tourists in their day-to-day interaction in English.

On the other hand, while asking the people to indicate the negative elements of tourism, the respondents from the community expressed their dissatisfaction mentioning that due to tourists' arrival, people have every chance of being influenced by their foreign cultures. The bad side of tourism also includes exposure to international crimes including drug trafficking and prostitution. The local people also often blame the tourists of being arrogant, insolent and often show disrespectfulness to the local culture. Most importantly, the pressure of tourism compels the depletion of natural resources; many roads and highways are built unnecessarily having negative impact on the environment in general.

Table 9: Positive aspects of tourism as understood by the Community People

• Increases the flow of economy.
• Increases job opportunities.
• Introduces Malaysian science and technology system.
• Malaysia can be introduced to the world.
• More exposure to other cultures.
• The entry of foreign currency.
• Intimate with foreigners.
• Learning good speaking skills with outsiders.
• Can learn their languages.
• Teaches to be friendly and tolerant of outsiders

Table 10: In general, the Negative aspects of tourism as assessed by the Respondents

• Possibility of being influenced by social interaction with the visitors.
• The culture of tourists often affect Malaysians
• Often committing criminal activities.
• Malaysia becomes crowded and thus becomes more exposed to environmental pollution.
• Price of basic necessities goes up.
• Outsiders are arrogant, insolent and disrespectful to the local norms
• Tourism may also allow drug trafficking and encourage prostitution.

As the respondents admitted to the economic impacts of tourism, the community people are asked to specify as to how they could increase their economic earning. Several specifications are mentioned in their viewpoints which are shown below. One of the points they noted is that the tourists most often purchase many food and other items from petty sellers which is an advantage for the local people.

Table 11
Respondents' Perception as to how the Earnings of the local people increases due to Tourism

Purchase our food which allows the expansion of business.
Foreigners do a lot of shopping which eventually increases Malaysian economy.
The foreigners buy local goods.
Some visitors develop business which increases production.
Foreign investment
Buying souvenirs.

Table 12
Observed Transformations that occur due to tourism

Many buildings such as shopping centers are built to attract the visitors
Positive emphasis on infrastructural development
The economy of the country progresses further
Development and refinement of the tourist places
Malaysia becomes more crowded.
A flow of foreign currency which seems good for the economy.
Improved transportation system.
Malaysia is exposed to more diversity.
Exposure to other cultures.
Malaysia becomes more famous in the world.

Tourism transforms the life and living of the community and hence, the respondents were asked to specify as to what sort of changes they usually notice due to ongoing tourism in Malaysia. A number of observations are enlisted which say that due to tourism many buildings such as, shopping centers are built in the country to attract people from outside. Due to tourism, many tourist spots are often renovated and refined to make them attractive. They also felt that due to tourism, the economy of the country develops further and after same time, transport and communication systems also improve to provide convenience to the tourists in their travels. Although these are apparent observations regarding infrastructural development, community people had many other views as well. They further said that due to tourism, Malaysia becomes known to others abroad and also at the same time, the country is exposed to other cultures.

To be exposed to other cultures is good from social interaction perspective, but it has many negative aspects which had been highlighted by the people interviewed in this research. The local people are often concerned about the visitors wearing non-Islamic attires which might influence the locals. It is further stated that being fascinated by the diversity, people often get acculturated which is not acceptable for a country like Malaysia where people maintain Islamic principles and Asian values.

Table 13
Cultural constraints of tourism as Viewed by the Respondents

• Malaysia moves into multiculturalism by ignoring their own values.
• Foreigners wear non-Islamic attire which looks unacceptable in the Malaysian culture.
• Losing own culture and people often become fascinated to the differences.
• Some places like the central part of the town become crowded and get dirty.
• Create noise.
• Damage the leads with the cultures.
• Less environmentally damaging.

Table 14
Environmental impacts of tourism as assessed by the Respondents

• It creates environmental pollution
• Social disease
• The cities and towns become more crowded
• Decreases natural resources
• Traffic jams
• Air pollutions
• Destroy the hills and forests in the name of development
• Water pollution

Chapter 6

Tourism In Malaysia: Controversial Viewpoints Based On Community People's Assessment

This chapter focuses on the positive and negative impacts of tourism by analyzing the qualitative data gathered through in-depth interviews and FGDs by relating them with supporting literatures and evidence. It shows the development of tourism in Malaysia by using scientific approach to identify the socio-economic, cultural and environmental impacts. These effects are viewed and explained from diverse perspectives by using local people's opinions, tourists' opinions and also a few experts' opinions. These views and explanations highlight tourism development in Malaysia as a controversial issue as a number of positive and negative disputes arise from this industry. Thus tourism in Malaysia has become a debatable issue concerning many people in the community.

Tourism in Malaysia and controversial roles of tourism from insiders' perspectives

ECONOMIC IMPACTS

The impacts of tourism on societal life is questionable and debatable, especially the environmental impacts which are generated from tourism. These debates cause the researchers to conduct research from multidisciplinary angles. At the beginning of human society, people considered nature as a dangerous and scary part of the world. People of that time did not dare to touch and utilize the natural resources. However, that tendency changed gradually and people started to consider nature as good for civilization. People started to utilize natural resources for their betterment. Natural resources like water, gas or minerals were extracted but then they did not have any consideration of the negative impacts of over- utilizing the natural resources. Now we can see a third trend of using natural resources. People today are concerned about the negative impact of overextracting natural resources while at the same time other people are focusing on the benefits of utilizing natural resources.

Like many other countries, Malaysian policy-makers are also more interested in getting economic profit from tourism. To give a long term economic advantage for the country, policy makers- consider tourism as one of the key sectors (Tang, 2015). In another paper by Tang and his associates, tourism is considered as one of the economic profit-oriented service sector of the world. But they add that Malaysian policy-makers place much emphasis on tourism sector, considering it as one of the potential sectors to establish Malaysia as a developed country. However, they regret that tourism fails to bring profit like agriculture or manufacturing sectors of Malaysia (Tang &Tan, 2015).

Globalization is a key contributor in increasing economic profit from tourism. However, according to some researchers (e.g., Antonakakis, Dragouni &Filis, 2015), tourism cannot provide a stable economy of a country; rather the amount of economic profit coming from tourism varies from time to time. Though no one can ignore the fluctuation of economic profit, still the most attractive impact of tourism on society is its capacity to bring in economic revenue. The most interesting part of tourism is, other impacts generated from tourism such as environmental change or socio-cultural change take place in a slow speed and thus the general public and even the government are less concerned about these impacts. The Malaysian government and policy-makers are not exceptional. These authorities treated tourism as a machine of economic growth without considering other related impacts (Awang, 2010).

Because of its economic productivity, some researchers (i.e. Byström & Müller, 2014) prefer to consider tourism as a commodity which is able to produce preferred economic reimbursements. These researchers suggest protecting the attractive part of a country to capture the tourists' attention which can bring regional development to that country.

Malaysia is rich in its natural resources such as tin, rubber, petroleum, palm oil or even timber and wood. These resources differentiate Malaysia from other countries which do not have these natural resources. To diversify its natural resources and source of economy, this country focuses on tourism. Many earlier researchers believed that the recent fall of Malaysian economy can be enhanced positively through globalized and comprehensive tourism services (Awang, 2010). In support of globalized tourism services of Malaysia, Awang (2010) further adds that Malaysia has 29 international offices which promote Malaysian tourism to the world outside. Through these international offices, Malaysia tries to gain the interest of tourists who farvaur multi-cultural is in which persuades the government to utilize the unused and fallow areas of Malaysia such as Langkawi and a few other islands. However, he cautions that putting much attention to some tourist-oriented places and allocating much budget these areas may allow deprivation and unfair development policies for other non-tourist oriented places. Many researchers like Brohman (1996) suggest applying appropriate tourism policies to avoid unwanted socio-ecological problems due to rapid growth of tourism.

Malaysian rural livelihood is mostly based on agricultural and stock which provide peoplewith limited options in earning and inability to bring in economic development like its urban counterparts. To kindle its development, it is urgent to look for alternatives and policy-makers suggest tourism as an alternative. According to these policy-makers, by utilizing local resources, tourism can provide diversified source of livelihoods and incomes which definitely will enhance rural development. Malaysian tourism policies must focus on spreading tourism among the rural communities to reduce rural poverty but Liu (2006) in his empirical research on the people of Kedah to justify their involvement with tourism, found a far distan involvement between these two variables. In his paper, he states, "results indicate that the current development irony arises because of the insufficient attention to local capacity building, reluctance to integrate local settlements and a misplaced notion of professionalism. Insensitivity to cater for cultural and ethnic differences in the encounters of host and guest also impedes meaningful local involvement" (Liu, 2006: p. 878). Liu agrees that though economically tourism gives some advantages to the rural Muslims, Kedah people are not trained and are not culturally prepared to entertain tourists coming from various parts of the world. These authors prefer to say that development that is apparently visible in Kedah is the fulfillment of political will where the rich and elites are getting advantages in building the infrastructure bringing ultimate ruin to the local culture. This situation may also be true for Kelantan where the people are more conservative and discourage tourists with their western cultures and attitudes from visiting their land.

Tourism has brought immense infrastructural development to Malaysia (Musa, 2000). To attract overseas tourism, the government of Malaysia has paid much attention in developing roads and highways, hotels and other private sectors' development. Musa (2000) mentions that private sectors development includes improvement hotels and lodgings and other tourist related conveniences. Apart from these, to support the private sectors, ample workforce is considered as a vital and necessary activity. At the same time, encouraging the local Malay people to participate in tourism activities is not a small priority for tourism development. To include local Malays tourism projects, Malaysia's diversified lifestyle with multiple ethnic groups is considered the first and foremost thing to demonstrate to the outside tourists. Malaysia with its multiple ethnic groups is rich in its culture including festivals, religious occasions, architectural beauties with high rise buildings, mosques and temples, diversified cuisine and life styles. With its natural and architectural beauty, Malaysia has built a number of theme parks which attract both the local and international tourists (Musa, 2000).

Chan (2015) in his book states that the second largest foreign currency generation sector of Malaysia is tourism. He agrees without controversy that Tourism Malaysia is boosting its economic development and economic prosperity but at the same time, he encourages green tourism as this type of tourism can bring sustainable development by avoiding the negative impact on local culture and environment.

Insider's view on tourism and its economic impacts:

Faiza, a highly educated researcher in Malaysia, said that "tourism has controversial role for our society. For economic growth it works very positively. In running the economic profit from tourism, extension of urban places increased a lot than before which provides employment for many people in the country".

Shazeea, an administrative staff of a government organization, mentioned that "of course tourism brings positive contribution to our economy since it enhances local investment and local employment which has good contribution in overall country's economy". Yet, Shazeea reminded us, pointing out the negative aspect of it when she says that "sometimes tourism is responsible for increasing the price of products by creating pressure on local economy." From this perspective, she is quite right in her statement as tourism has commercial attraction in Malaysia but simultaneously, due to presence of foreign customers the price of goods goes up. For example, KLCC is the pride of Malaysia but Malaysian people rarely can buy products from there of high prices of many international brand products; whereas, the Europeans and the Arabs can afford to buy these things. These kinds of psychological deprivation sometimes make us down". She goes on to say that we cannot however deny that such commercial transaction keeps the economy flourished and buyer's spending money in Malaysia intact in that context.

Nurul Farhana, a Master's student who has worked as an NGO staff before, stated "tourism has definitely some negative impact on societal life but for Malaysia, tourism mostly does benefit for our country. It exposes the local product and the people to the outsiders. It is good mostly from economical perspectives. It helps the local businessman and investors to be exposed in front of the international tourists".

She added, "the highest negative and positive both impacts goes on economic perspectives. It is true tourism brings economic benefits but that is mostly for the government directly but not the local people. For example to attract the tourist government focuses only on the capital city or the urban areas. In contrast though many tourist spots are in remote areas and to support these tourists people of those areas had managed themselves and get benefits. But government takes the responsibility to support the tourists and makes high rise infrastructure, hotels and other supports. However, the local already made home stay and others. This is how tourism is killing the opportunity for the local benefits".

Azuzana, a lecturer in a private college, said "in terms of economy, tourism in Malaysia is very positive. Every year Malaysia earns a lot of revenue from tourism sector. Gas and mining is the first sector which earns the highest revenue each year and after that the second highest revenue comes from tourist sector".

Analysis: Malaysia is a fast growing country where tourism plays an important role. It is considered as the second highest remittance earner sector for Malaysian economy. Malaysia has vast resources to attract tourists from around the world. To attract tourists to come and enjoy Malaysia, the government has to first focus on developing the infrastructure in thecountry. In developing doing the infrastructure to support tourism, Malaysia has to utilize its jungle resources. Fast growing urbanism with high rise buildings, modern hotels and restaurants, shopping malls and even long-wide highways have replaced our jungles. These modern infrastructures allow investors to invest in Malaysia which bring new windows of economic profit for the country. Tourism is opening opportunities for all parties to invest. Investors are attracted to do business as they can promote their products to many customers from different countries at one time. Local investors can also promote local products to many customers to justify their products and tastes. For example, islands and beaches are mostly in remote areas of Malaysia but these are hot spots for tourists. Thus, local villagers are getting the chance to invest in "home stay" which enables them to benefit economically. Thus tourism generates prospects for Malaysian outlay in other countries also. These investments increase local employment which in turns increases the overall economic development of the country.

Malaysia is a Southeast Asian country which is rich in terms of its natural beauty. To have an instant advantage from this natural beauty, the country has to develop the tourism sector to attract people of different taste from around the world. The advantage mostly comes from economic profit. It is well accepted that the economy is such an important indicator of development which help to bring sustainable development to a country. Thus tourism helps to fulfill the basic demands of humanity with economic profit.

Globalization and tourism are interlinked concepts. When globalization received an international acceptance, many countries like Malaysia tried to be part of globalization through tourism. This participation was mostly one way where Malaysia opened its door in welcoming people from around the world. Thus, tourism of Malaysia creats a big market to the outsiders where Malaysia can promote all its resources including natural to commercial ones.

Tourism becomes a process of development which needs continuous renovation of infrastructure. This certainly positively impacts the economy through creating options in investment.

Social Impacts of Tourism

Social impacts of tourism mean the effects on the traditional life style of a society through tourism. These impacts are always negative on the cultural life, it cannot be justified, and rather some impacts caused by tourism are certainly good for society. Economic impacts are very noticeable compared to social impacts but the value system of the host country or its family structure, communal relationship. These changes occur through the interaction of locals with the tourists. Researchers (e.g. Mathieson & Wall, 1982) state that if the socio-economic background of the tourists and their hosts country differ strongly then the chance to be influenced by the tourists is high. But along with association between members of the host country and the tourists, the other important reason for cultural change in the host country is a tourism-based industrial enlargement (Rátz, 2000). Mbaiwa (2005) assesses the socio-cultural impacts of tourism on the Okavango Delta people of Botswana. Though he used both secondary and primary methods of data collection, he claimed his research was mostly based on a survey. The findings of the data from his research show both the positive and negative impacts of tourism development on the socio-cultural life of the society. According to his research findings, the positive impacts mostly occur because of infrastructural development due to tourism. However, along with many other negative impacts he talks about the increasing of crime rates, expansion of prostitution and embracing of other countrie's culture. More or less similar findings came from a recent book of Smith (2015) where he shows the impacts of tourism on Mali culture. Like Mbaiwa (2005), he also discovered both the positive and negative impacts of tourism on the traditional life style of the host country. In a case study, Smith (2015) shows that though Mali is one of the poorest countries in the world it is a hotspot for European tourists for its famous world heritage sites, culture such as music, dance and traditional handicrafts. According to this author, tourism creates a focus on the local communities and their cultures which work to strengthen their identity to the world. To keep this identity to the world, the host country always retains its traditions and uniqueness. This is how Mali people are selling their culture and presenting themselves with the world. But he warned with evidence that selling one's culture to the world through tourism is another way of destroying their sacred culture. The economic lure of progressing the country has eroded the local livelihood strategies and increased crime which clearly shows the gap between the economic and cultural sustainability.

Nejati Mohamed and Omar (2014) in their research discovered more positive social impacts compared to negative impacts. They outline that tourism development increases public facilities like roads and transport, the Internet and other modern communication system as developed in Perhentian Island and Redang Island of Malaysia. However, this article highlights that in both places social problems like sexual harassment, drug abuse and other criminal activities have also increased more than before. For that reason, the residents of those islands have very rightly, express their positive intuition by saying that through the tourism development they can expose their local cultures to the world of foreign culture. However, many of them are concerned about the extinction of local cultures and the absorbtion of foreign one's; especially western culture.

Faiza, a post graduate student from Malaysia said, "though from economical point of view, it has a lot of positive impacts but at the same time, it has many negative social impacts also. A lot of tourists are coming to Malaysia every year, many of them are bringing drugs and illegal things purposively. Apart from this, it has other negative impacts on social life also. Prostitutions reach at the corner of the country. Prostitution is not an urban problem anymore; it is a concern for the whole country. To support the tourists, many rural girls need to involve in prostitutions."

Shazeea, a government administrative staff, also talked about the negative impacts of tourism on social life. She said, "there are a number of negative impacts of tourism, especially on socio-cultural life. The foreign tourists eventually take a chance to come and visit Malaysia which allow them to go anywhere in the country. So, it is quite likely that illegal workers, illegal drug supplies and many other criminals also enter the country for their illegal activities". She added, "I am not sure how serious the administrators are about these cases. The foreigners those who come from outside Malaysia, they do not know the culture of Malaysia." However, she did not wanted to blame the tourists, rather she wanted the authority to be more responsible. She, thus said, "tourists are not entirely responsible in destroying our local culture Instead of tourists, the poor authority (mass media and entertainment media) integration is responsible for bringing vulgar culture from others".

Farhana stated "from cultural perspective, Malaysian people are trying to follow the tourists in many perspectives. For example, previously when tourism didn't start as a commercial business, during that time we have fix dress attire. But now as tourism becomes a big industry, not only the human being, their culture along with their dresses are also welcomed by the people of Malaysia. So this is how we are losing our own dress and attire gradually. So this is not true only for dresses rather other cultural part like language, food habit and others, we are trying to follow the outsiders, we are trying to be like them". She further suggested some policies to be designed from these by saying, "so for me, if we want to get rid of this, we need to educate our parents and need to aware them about the originality and uniqueness of our nation. But for this negative impact I don't want to blame the tourists. They came here because we welcome them to come. So we should be respectful towards their culture and movement. But it is our government, tourism ministry and individuals' responsibility to keep the boundary that what activities the tourists as a foreigner can enjoy here and what culture we can follow. For example, we should not allow the non-Muslim tourists to drink openly and at the same time as their culture is to drink so we should provide them restricted places".

Analysis: Like economical impacts, tourism has dual impacts on the socio-cultural life of the Malays. From the negative perspective, the locals are considering tourism as a threat to their culture. Some of the respondents believed if the government takes proper initiatives, the negative impacts can be avoided and they focused more on identifying the negative impacts so that proper policies can be adopted to run tourism without disturbance. For this reason, few respondents were concerned about the negative impacts of tourism such as spreading western culture among the youth by participating in night clubs or drinking alcohol like many tourists in Malaysia. These respondents were highly concerned about the fast spreading of prostitution or call girl culture among the local females who work mostly to support thmselves by entertaining the foreign clients. However, these respondents are very much positive in sharing and enjoying multi-cultural attire and food from multi-cultures to entertain tourists of various countries. Based on all these issues, the locals gave much importance on monitoring the tourism sector so that the Malaysian government can reduce the negative impacts of tourism in Malaysia.

Environmental Impacts:

The concern of tourism is measured from an extensive and multidisciplinary viewpoint which associates economic, psychological, geographical and sociological procedures (Ryan, 1991). In many countries, environmental protection and related policies are getting more prominence in tourism sector to bring sustainable environmental management. It is found that tourism has brought considerable impacts on natural and social environment which requires multidisciplinary study focusing on sustainable development. As Tourism Agenda 21 campaigns for considering the opinions of the host residents to bring development to the tourism industry, this part of the current chapter focuses on the local residents' views about the socio-environmental impacts that tourism brings into their society.

Throughout the history, people have a close connection with nature. Whenever people talk about tourism, the sight that comes to our mind is the image of nature including the sun, beaches, islands as well as food and shopping. Many researchers (Lis, 2009) argue that even if precautionary steps are taken against the negative impact of tourism, it cannot be avoided absolutely. They dispute that tourism will increase the normal usage of natural resources. Thus many empirical researches are indicating that even though Tourism Agenda 21 suggests considering for local residents' views and long term benefits for the host community, tourism still brings environmental problems despite the suggestions. Gao, Li, Fu, Zhu and Ding (2015) forecast that in the near future the environmental impacts through tourism will be more complicated and critical. Though earlier researchers were optimistic of the positive impacts of tourism but the trend of thinking has changed in recent times. The socio-anthropologists of the 1970s criticized the negative impacts of tourism on culture but now these groups are talking about environmental impacts of tourism. In their paper, they state that it is difficult to prove the local people's view whether they are wrong or right but it is important to take into considerations of their statement.

Tourism and nature are related solely where relaxing on an island is the second most preferable holiday for tourists. In his empirical research on Cayo Guillermmo, Gutierrez (2015) shows that appropriate technology is required to avoid ecological fragility created from tourism. He further states that tourism negatively affects on its air and soil by destroying its forests, including the wild habitats. Appropriate technology is needed to improve the drainage system of the islands and their surface water. He adds that tourism increases noise and air pollution through over-population and fast growth of urbanization. His research further talks about soil and water pollution of islands through tourism. Excessive exhaustion of sediment and dust into the sea water of the islands is reducing water quality. Not only that, tourism causes beach erosion and cutting of trees can cause entire degradation of any island. In his paper, he suggests for appropriate technology to avoid all these environmental impacts resulting from tourism.

Nejati, Mohamed and Omar (2014) conducted a research where they investigate the observations and awareness of the locals of two famous islands of Malaysia about the socio, economic, environmental and cultural impacts of tourism. By using a survey on the residents of Perhentian Island and Redang Island, the findings show that tourism has immense impacts on the environment as it destroys water quality and the bio diversity and reduces air quality.

Backhaus (2005) talks about ecological problems which according to him increase from too many flights carrying in touristsand are making up-down and the commercial industry that grows to support the tourists' communication.

Faiza said, "Urbanization increased a lot than before which cause negative impacts on country's forest resources. I never witnessed natural disasters like floods in my life time. But some months before country's devastating floods occurred in many parts of Malaysia. Now I think it is a time to rethink about tourism whether it is giving us sustainable support for the society or not".

Shazeea said "Environmental degradation is happening due to tourism, this statement is not true absolutely. We need to do more research on multidisciplinary work so that we can understand the relationship between environmental degradation and tourism in Malaysia. But apparently the climate of Malaysia has changed a lot which is clear through long dry season, sudden attack of floods, increased landslides and many more".

Farhana stated, "Tourism for me is a mix of positive and negative impacts. We need to consider the negative impacts and need to think about the future generation and only then we can enjoy the benefits from tourism. Timun Island of Terengganu which is rich in natural beauty is an attractive place for the tourists. So to care these tourists' local people with their local capacities made home stay, food court and other shelter centre with which both parties were satisfied. But once the government noticed that this place is an attraction for the tourists, government with their huge investment did a reconstruction without considering the local demand. They cut the forests and constructed big buildings and expanded the urban support for the tourists. So this is how tourism is causing unemployment problem for the locals and degrading the environment by cutting forests and constructing high rise buildings. For me, regarding pressure on living standard, it depends on the state. If you go Johor which is neighbor state of Singapore and Singaporean frequently visit Johor. Singaporean people has higher income and so when they visit Johor, they can buy anything whatever they want. So the local investor increased the price of everything which actually create pressure on local and general people. But other state even some parts of Kuala Lumpur which are not famous for tourism, their living expense is lower than the Johor people. This is true for me as I am original from Johor and residing in one part of Kuala Lumpur. Regarding recent flood of Malaysia, one of the reasons is taking sand from the river in an unplanned way. There is massive deforestation, though these places are not tourist oriented areas. Being a developed country, Malaysia is trying to stabilize the locals' economic standard but to do that the lower income people is paying a lot compare to the elite people. Government is focusing much on the elite people. In general, as a general people I must say that government should pay much attention on culture and environmental impact of tourism, together with the economic impacts, and only then sustainable development will come from Tourism sector of Malaysia".

Analysis: No studies, so far have ignored the positive impacts of tourism on socio-economic elements. This is mostly because of its positive results on local economies that improve local people's average income and quality of life, and cumulating investments in business commotion. It generates employment regardless of social class and other socio-demographic differences. Tourism opens accesses for outdoor opportunities by avoiding dependency on indoor activities. Like socio-economic aspect, many acknowledge the positive impacts of tourism on environmental sectors. The findings of this chapters supports that tourism has positive impacts from the environmental perspective also it creates awareness among the population that to gain socio-economic benefits from tourism, they need to preserve of their environment. Like other sectors, the environment also has received some negative impacts from tourism. According to the results found from the interviews, the insiders claimed that climate change is happening rapidly more than before in Malaysia. According to the interviewees, it is happening in Malaysia due to the over extraction of natural resources and extending of urban areas with high rise buildings, roads, highways and other infrastructural development. It was found that currently Malaysia is over-crowded, more than in any other decade of history. Urban pollution, islands pollution and even highland pollution become very obvious nowadays. Natural disasters occur frequently throughout the year. Devastating floods happened in 2014 and a year later shocking earthquake also occurred in this country. Haze has become a common and frequent problem for Malaysians. Climate change is so dominant in Malaysiaasas many parts of the country are experiencing water crisis during certain times of the year. Local people believe that these environmental problems may have a link with over extension of tourism without implementing the appropriate policies.

TOURISM IN MALAYSIA FROM OUTSIDERS' PERSPECTIVES:

Case 1:

Respondent's Name: Fatima
Age: 55 years old
Occupation: Housewife
Nationality: Palestinian

I came to Malaysia because my children stay in Malaysia, so I came to visit them. I will stay about 17 days in a rented apartment. In the mean time, I visited many places such as Port Dickson, Genting Highland, Kuala Lumpur City Centre (KLCC), Cameron Highlands, Sunway Lagoon, Putra Jaya, Malacca, China Town, Melawati Hills. I visited all these places because of the reason that I heard about these places which are suitable for enjoyment and relaxation as some of my friends came to Malaysia and recommended me to visit these places. Another reason for me to visit these places is that these places are not costly. Nature: Nature is very beautiful. Green trees are everywhere, it is like a heaven. I live in Saudi Arabia when I go from place to place, normally I travel in the desert, I do not see the trees like here. Weather: also is better than Saudi Arabia because it is warm not cool, no need to use heavy clothes, another issue is there is no dust like Saudi Arabia, I feel here the atmosphere is cleaner and more healthy. It is true the humidity is high but in general it is better than where I stay in Saudi Arabia. High-rise building: When I look from the window I see the highest building in Malaysia and a lot of other buildings around it, the view is fantastic, I like the way how the Malaysians organize their buildings to make the city beautifully organized. People: In fact I did not interact with the local people and this is because I do not understand their language and also because I stay here for a short period of time but what I notice especially when I use the train as a new experience, everyone in Malaysia is totally independent from the other, for example no one looks at any one in terms of how the other addresses himself, I feel everyone is busy with something not like us in Saudi Arabia the woman cannot go even to the street alone and if she does she will face many challenges and disturbances from other people in the street especially gazing at her even though she cover from top to toe. culture: I do not know. I do not have any interaction with any local. Food: In fact I do not like the Malaysian food at all, I went many times to different malls and I saw different kinds of Malaysian food and I tried some but I do not like it at all. In fact Malaysia is naturally beautiful, the Creator gives Malaysia natural beauty, and the Malaysian leaders organize this beauty to make the country more beautiful even though Malaysia is not a rich country like Gulf countries such as Saudi Arabia. For example, Saudi Arabia is much richer than Malaysia many times but Malaysia looks more developed and advanced than Saudi Arabia in terms of transportation, and communications, services at the petrol stations and post offices. But to be honest, if Malaysians want to improve their country they must improve some issues such as, security: Related to this issue for example, I lost my hand bag inside the airport before I check in my luggage, and directly we contacted many departments inside the airport to find the bag, but unfortunately they told me they do not find it, in fact I do not even feel they are serious to find it, they just say wait and we will call back and I think like these mistakes will affect negatively this country. They have to show more care for customer services. Food: Also Malaysians should improve the quality of their food or facilitate to people who come from different countries to open international restaurants because tourists need their own food, and this will encourage people to come to Malaysia. I have been told that there are many Arab restaurants here but having a meal with the family in one of these restaurants may cost RM300. Of course, if anyone asks me about the country I will encourage him or she to visit Malaysia, and the reason is clear the beauty of the country and prices are affordable.

Case: 2

Name: Nisreen
Age: 37 years old
Occupation: Housewife
Nationality: Saudi Arabia

This is the first time I travel abroad, my mother came to Malaysia three times and she talked a lot about Malaysia and its beauty, I was hoping to come one day to visit Malaysia especially my sister and her family stay in Malaysia and they know many things about the country. I will stay here one month as I got visa for one month only. I will stay at an apartment nearby Kuala Lumpur city. I visit many places such as Port Dickson, Genting Highland, Kuala

Lumpur City Centre KLCC, Cameron Highlands, Sunway Lagoon, Putra Jaya, Melaka, China Town, Melawati Hills. I visit all these places because everyone who came to Malaysia talked about these places and their beauty, in Saudi Arabia there is a habit now, if anyone wants to marry he should visit Malaysia to make the honeymoon there because they believe it is not costly, so when they come back they start to show the photos that they pick up in Malaysia in different places. In fact these photos encouraged me a lot to come and visit Malaysia. The nature: I like the Malaysian nature so much green color everywhere, wherever you go you are in the garden, trees, flowers everywhere especially when I went to Genting highlands and used the skyway, the view was amazing, the trees with the green color cover everything. The weather: I like the weather also so much especially because there is no dust, the weather is warm the tourist can make a tour comfortably without thinking with the cool weather, even when it rains, it rains for one or two hours then it stops without cool and when it stops I feel as the city has been washed without any floods comparing with what happens in Saudi Arabia, just little raining make floods and the whole city becomes in a miss. High-rise building: I like the view of the buildings when I look from my room, but I think in the future it will not be beautiful if the Malaysian built a lot of buildings, the beauty of Malaysia comes from the trees and the green colors not from increasing the number of buildings which will make the city very crowd. People: I do not interact with the local people here. Culture: I do not know. Food: I do not like it and the smell is not good. Food: Malaysian must improve the quality of their food and find people to open international restaurants to offer international food because people have the stereotype that Malaysia an Islamic country, and this is way they prefer to come here comparing with Thailand and China, so Malaysian should understand this issue and facilitate to the tourists such as Gulf countries the food they used to eat by opening Arab restaurants. Security: While I arrived to Malaysia and left the airport to my sister's home I felt I am not secure because I did not see the Malaysian soldiers in the streets like I used to see in our countries soldiers with their automatic guns everywhere, but when my relatives show me the CCTV cameras in the streets I like this idea more than spreading soldiers with weapons in the streets, but at the same time my relatives told me the city is not safe and I have to be alert from people who snatch bags or phones. I hope to come again to visit Malaysia with my family next time, and I will encourage anyone to come and visit Malaysia, as the country is not very costly.

Analysis: Outsiders view tourism in Malaysia as quite interesting and their views are very much similar to the insiders' view. Their perception regarding the impact of tourism in Malaysia can be related with the insiders' views. From the cultural perspective, it is observed that tourists have little chance of mingling with the locals and with their cultures. Both parties mostly avoid each other due to language barrier. Not only language, food intake causes a barrier in knowing locals culture. According to the outsiders it is advisable to have more international restaurants with cheap price. However, it may cause a threat on local food culture and local investors. The result also proves the claim of the insiders that entering Malaysia with tourists' visa is easy and cheap causing illegal staying of many foreigners which may cause a threat on the local security. If the positive impacts are taken into consideration, it can be found that the greenery and the natural beauty of Malaysia are attracting tourists from all over the world, thus needs much protection for sustainable development.

CASE 3: EXPERT'S OPINION ABOUT THE IMPACT OF TOURISM IN MALAYSIA

Dr. Nor Azlin Binti Tajuddin (PhD from UWA, Australia)
Assistant Professor
Department of Sociology and Anthropology
International Islamic University Malaysia (IIUM)

QUESTION 1: Should the government of Malaysia encourage tourism at a larger extent in the country?

Generally, of course, the Malaysian government should further support tourism industries as it is one of the main contributors to Malaysian GDP which is parallel with the world economic growth. I think the tourism sector also steadily contributes to the world economy at least in the recent decade. Emergence of low cost airlines like Air Asia could further accelerate the tourism industries in Asian continent in general and Malaysia in particular. Travelling has become easier and cheaper nowadays, so, it is better to join the race. In fact, in Asian region, we have new competitor like Vietnam is catching up very fast to become one of the favorite tourist destinations.

QUESTION 2: What are the better sides of tourism and what kind of tourists can be patronized in Malaysia?

As mentioned earlier, tourism contributes a lot to our economic growth. That is the most obvious positive sides of tourism. For general public, it generates a lot of jobs like in airlines services, hotel and management, home cottage industries like souvenirs, batik, etc, leisure services. For me, I'm concerned about the direct benefit to the local people. Take a look at Langkawi and even Kota Bahru you can see there are lots of homestay services offered to tourists. There would also be a great demand for local food and craft. So these would help the local people to earn extra income especially with the current price hikes in Malaysia.

Another good thing about tourism is that we can expect physical infrastructure and facilities will be upgraded to attract tourists and in turn the spill effect will be enjoyed by the local people. We went for a family day in Pangkor Island during Chinese New Year holiday recently. The first time I visited the island when I was 10 years old. That was 3 decades back. Back then there was only an old jetty to transfer both local and tourists from Lumut to the island. But now you have two jetties – Pulau Pangkor and Marina. Mind you, these are not jetties *per se* but actually business/leisure complexes ... you can find eateries, convenience stores, marine products shops, bathrooms, *surau* (prayer room for the Muslims) etc here.

What kind of tourism can be patronized here?

As tourists, people come to Malaysis from various backgrounds – nationalities, ethnicity, socio-economic status, etc. So naturally we need to offer a variety of activities of tourism packages. We can have beach, outdoor adventure, historical/cultural and ecotourism packages. As Malaysia is surrounded by beaches, definitely, beach holiday should be our main product tourism product. Outdoor adventure tourism is like you do white-water rafting in Selangor or Ulu Slim Rivers, climbing Mount Kinabalu, cave exploration of Gua Niah.

Historical/cultural tourism is for people who like to visit arts, museums or historical sites such as Malacca. Lastly, ecotourism, in a way its similar to outdoor adventure tourism in which you are out there visiting natural wonder. I think there's misconception of the term ecotourism used in our country. Based on my observation and readings, here, in Malaysia, as long as you visited natural places then it is regarded as eco-tourism. Of course, visiting pristine or relatively untouched environment is one aspect of eco-tourism. But the most important aspect is to what extent these eco-tourism activities, services, etc. are sustainable ....? which do not jeopardize the pristine nature of the those natural places? Its supposed to be an educational experience to the tourists rather than merely aesthetical appreciation. For me ideally, it should even empowered those tourists in turn to protect those natural places that they have visited.

QUESTION 3: Negative aspects of tourism?

Everything in this world has both negative and positive sides. The key word is to do things moderately. As a nature lover, my concern would be the negative impacts on the environment. We need to think about a carrying capacity of a tourist spot - Too much development, too many hotels, gold resorts. Overcrowding tourists subsequently could generate hundred million tons of waste – all of these could be harmful for our environment.

We have to be careful, weigh our options. For example, for a small country like Malaysia with limited land spaces, do we really need more than 200 golf resorts? I know it brings good return for the economy but is it environmentally sustainable?

As a social scientist, I care about the local people. Social Impact Assessment needs to be done prior to any development especially mega tourism project. Personally, I'm wondering how construction of gold resort would bring greater benefit to the local people. I know it generates millions of RM for our country. Not to mention the land need to be cleared to accommodate this resort.

QUESTION 4: Environmental impacts of tourism? Please tell your viewpoint as an expert on environment.

We need to do a life-cycle analysis for any tourism packages or projects especially those places which have been gazetted as environmentally sensitive areas in order to assess the environmental impacts so that we can minimize the hazardous impacts.

First of all, you need to consider from the early stage of the planning to develop an area as a tourist destination i.e. the construction stage. Massive construction of a pristine undisturbed environment can create long lasting environmental impacts to the eco-system; say for example, construction of hotels, roads, gold resorts.

I think Malaysia has a tendency to erect or build the 6-star infrastructures, the biggest of anything the tallest building, the best resorts and all these which apparently seem to be attractive. But we have to think about the impact these on environments. Thus, we need to provide minimum infrastructure to provide basic facilities to the visitors of those environmentally sensitive areas. I visited quite a number of natural parks or pristine environments throughout the years in Australia, Switzerland, Turkey, Italy and the latest Plitvice National Park in Croatia last month. Most of these places provide minimum number of hotels and other infrastructure to assist the tourists. Moreover, they tried to develop the areas sustainably. For example, I'm very impressed with the construction of walk board, steps/ladders, signboards in Plitvice National as they were made of trees and branches found in the park itself!

Another thing, you need to consider the carrying capacity of a tourist spot. I hope there are environmental engineers or scientists out there who really look into this matter. Too many visitors can destroy the pristine nature ...say for example those beautiful corals and aquatic species in Pulau Redang. Have we done enough to educate those tourists of possible impacts that they may have on the environment?

Talking about the impact of visitors on Redang Island or Sipada Island and others, have we designed an efficient waste disposal system to minimize the impact on beaches or water bodies? I don't have answer to these questions but these should be our great concern.

QUESTION 5: Eco-tourism should be preferable to tourism in context to preserving the nature in Malaysia. Please tell us your viewpoint as an environmental specialist.

According to a report, eco-tourism is becoming the fastest growing form of tourism in Malaysia. Of course, ideally, if everything is done accordingly, eco-tourism should be able to preserve our natural heritage. My concern is whether we are taking any steps to make it sustainable both socially and environmentally.

As I mentioned earlier, many people – government, visitors, operators, or even mass media misinterpret the term eco-tourism as merely involve visiting natural pristine areas. What about other criteria – the need to minimize the impact of tourism activities, promoting environmental education/awareness, environmental preservation and preservation of local cultures? There is a global concern that there should be a regulatory body to monitor operators or self-acclaimed eco-tourism destinations. To what extent they really uphold the spirit of eco-tourism in a real sense? For this reason, I support this effort of accreditation. But unfortunately, I think there's no such effort in Malaysia as there is no requirement of procuring a general or HALAL certificate in buying organic product, vegetables or any other products.

Malaysia is blessed as one of mega-biodiversity countries in the world with it tropical rainforest and its hundreds species of flora and fauna. Our shores are homes to thousands aquatic species. Yes, we have lots to offer, thus, responsibilities to balance between tourism development and environmental preservation.

We need to further develop new eco-tourism product is like environmental volunteerism. We invite tourists to become volunteers to preserve those pristine places. Currently, I'm very pleased as we have tourist volunteers programs like Turtle Conservation and Orang Utan. Such efforts should further be encouraged and given higher allocation by the government rather than constructing of golf resort.

QUESTION 6: What are the socio-cultural impacts of tourism?

The socio-cultural impacts of tourism could be observed on the local communities first as they experienced the physical changes of the development and second as they interacted with the tourists. Say for example, we build a hotel deep in the rainforest which was previously occupied by the aborigines. As a result to accommodate these changes, the aborigines have to sacrifice their way of life such as their economic activities, cost of living, settlement pattern and maybe even their family institution, value systems and other cultural heritage.

The local people could be exposed to the values and morality of the tourists which may contradict with those of the locals. For instance, the selling and consumption of liquor in a Muslim dominated area like in Langkawi. The impacts might be very subtle and hard to measure, though.

In other situations, to some extent, tourism could protect local culture and traditions. As I mentioned previously, there's always two sides of a coin. I observed the making of shape – a traditional musical instrument when I visited Sarawak Cultural Village last year. So it's good as you preserve this material culture. And in turn material culture could strengthen our ethnic or identities.

Overall viewpoints about tourism in Malaysia

I think Malaysia needs an overriding or overarching principle/s that guide its booming tourism industry which are consistent and not contradicting with one another. This is what had happened in Langkawi. On one hand, we have a Langkawi GeoPark Heritage and on the other we Langkawi as a Shopping Paradise – duty free centre. Do you know that we have more than 10 shopping complexes in a small island like Langkawi? We don't go shopping for our basic needs when we are on vacation. We shop for luxuries or unnecessary/ excess goods. You encourage (unlimited) consumerism. Principally it's just not right. If you are a marketing strategist, the branding it's just not right, it's inconsistent. You can create identity confusion! I mean … I can understand if you want to promote cities like KL as a shopping paradise but please not in Langkawi or any other 'pristine' natural places.

And I hope eco-tourism and cultural heritage should be the main tourism products of Malaysia rather than shopping and gold tourisms.

Chapter 7

Conclusions, Findings And Recommendations For Future Protection

This study on tourism is an empirical research based on collecting primary data through quantitative and qualitative investigations of an urban community located in Klang Valley in Kuala Lumpur, Malaysia. As part of its theoretical investigation, the research critically reviewed and analysed enormous literature, books, reports and articles on tourism at the national and international levels. These reviewed materials along with empirical information have directed us to conceptualize the scope of tourism in Malaysia and also have developed in us a worldview and guidelines for tourism research in this country. Since tourism has been expanding nationally and internationally, we have provided in this report a worldview on tourism which will eventually help us to conceptualize a broad paradigm and guideline for tourism research in Malaysia.

The research generated data on visitors who have arrived in Malaysia from at least 22 foreign countries covering four different continents showing their special fascination for Malaysian tourism. Visitors' evaluation indicates that they liked Malaysia for several reasons as they find the country as peaceful and politically stable; simultaneously they also rated the people here as cordial and helpful. It is therefore recommended that the government and policy planners in Malaysia provide proper direction to popularize tourism and, they must also take all sorts of precaution to preserve the natural environment to create an ecological balance in the country.

Local people's perception of tourism in Malaysia seems to be quite logical to visualize the trends in tourists' arrival and also at the same time, it is essential to have an idea about the type of people who are making trips to this country for a shorter duration. Contextually, we sketch here a background profile of the visitors coming to Malaysia and produce a sense of reconciliation to bring them together for a socio-cultural and economic interaction. In view of this consideration, a total of 150 tourists from 23 different countries including 25 Malaysians from other areas of the country were identified and interviewed. They have been visited Klang Valley and its surrounding places in Kuala Lumpur. It is reflected from our data that apart from visitors coming from a number of Asian countries, visitors also came from West Europe, Middle-East, Australia, Canada and the United States. While talking to these visitors very informally during the interviews, it has been ascertained that the tourists are exceedingly happy and satisfied with the treatment they receive here from the local people. Most of the respondents regard Malaysia as climatically and geographically suitable and ethno-politically a peaceful country.

It has been mentioned earlier that Malaysians in general do not pose much negative attitude to foreign visitors and this has been proven when we find that 87% of the respondents from two communities of Taman Impian Ehsan and Taman Midah mentioned that they like tourists visiting their country. With a view to identify the reasons for which they like tourists visiting their country, a series of responses emerged. These are: (a) economic transaction increases; (b) Malaysia becomes known to other persons; (c) people can learn foreign languages and get acquainted with their cultures; (d) it is proven that Malaysia is a right and conducive place to visit and so on.

The community people have ideas about the good and bad effects of tourism. When asked to identify the good effects of tourism, most of them mentioned that it increases the flow of economy and simultaneously enhances job opportunities for the local people. Then there are other views saying that the local people get exposure to other cultures and also they have a feeling that the arrival of more tourists into the country indicates that Malaysia gets introduced to many nations of the world. In regard to its utility, the community people also think that it allows the people to learn foreign language which makes them particularly proficient in English as they have to communicate with the tourists in their day-to-day interaction.

On the other hand, while asking the people to indicate the bad effects of tourism, the respondents from the community expressed their dissatisfaction that due to tourists' arrival, people have every chance of being influenced by the foreign cultures. The bad effects of tourism also include exposure to international crimes having allowed drug trafficking and encouraged prostitution. The local people also often blame some tourists of being arrogant, insolent and often show disrespect to the local culture. Most importantly, the pressure of tourism compels the depletion of natural resources; many roads and highways are built unnecessarily having negative impact on the environment in general.

It has already been mentioned that tourism has become one of the fastest growing industries in the world. There are multiple factors for such increase including (i) modern and globalized communication system, (ii) increasing education and attitudinal views, looking at life and cultures are main factors among others. Due to fast development and modernization, there has been an increase in the number of tourists arriving from all over the world. When people move from one place to another it may not always be part of recreation, it has also good and bad effects.

The socio-economic, cultural and environmental impacts of tourism in Malaysia have been explained from diverse perspectives: by using local people's opinion, tourists' assessment and also based on an experts' opinion. These views and explanation cause tourism in Malaysia a controversial issue of development as a number of positive and negative aspects arise from this industry. Another word, tourism in Malaysia has become a debatable issue concerning many people in the community. Malaysia is quite rich with natural resources which attract many tourists to visit and view its beauty. For these tourists, an independent tourism industry has flourished which supports them by giving social security, infrastructural support and other legal assistance, thus this industry is getting benefit economically. In a sense, it will not be a wrong to say that 'tourism industry is selling Malaysia's natural beauty to get economic prosperity'. It should be mentioned that the number of local tourists who travel across Malaysia is not negligible but the tourism industry of Malaysia is highly dependent on foreign tourists.

The first attraction for international tourists in Malaysia is its easy location and being central from the geographical point of view. Easy access of visa as compared to many other western nations is one of the major causes for thriving popularity of Malaysian tourism. The friendly attitude of Malaysians is also a key factor for foreigners to choose Malaysia as a choice for a visit. Yet we cannot deny the fact that the basic cause for Malaysian tourism is its natural beauty. Malaysia is famous for its islands and highlands; it is also known for its tolerable and moderate climate, attracting the foreigners especially from Europe and North America where they mostly have to stay in long winter. For that reason, they come to these areas to relax and enjoy the nature. In this context, Malaysia is trying to give its highest infrastructural support to make every corner of the country enjoyable to the tourists. To enjoy the nature, tourists are going far into the remote parts of Malaysia, like Sabah and Sarawak.

To make tourism industry more available to tourists, Malaysia extends its focus on to man-made attractions along with its natural beauty. Malaysia has been trying to combine the artificial beauty with the existing natural beauty which successfully enables Malaysia to attract more tourists in this country. Moreover, socio-politically Malaysia is a liberal and friendly country which allows foreigners to come and enjoy their vacation comfortably to overcome their monotonous life. Malaysian culture is also versatile that even the locals feel interested to travel around in various parts of Malaysia. Culturally, Malaysia is a multi-racial and multi-ethnic country. Thus, it has rich cultural resources which attract various groups of tourists to know and discover Malaysia. Tourism of Malaysia thus helps tourists to mix with the locals and share the culture of each other, enabling them to learn the culture of different ethnic groups in one country.

Tourism department in Malaysia often shows in the billboard advertising Malaysia possessing all features of true Asia; it however, is not an exaggeration as it preserves all traditional cultures in the modern forms. People in Malaysia are religious, but not fanatic. Muslim cultures are prioritized but side by side, other cultures are well-respected. Even having Muslim dominance, western people and tourists get all facilities in Malaysia required for their everyday life. While visiting KLCC or Bukit Bintang and a few areas in the down town of Kuala Lumpur, the tourists and the visitors from western cultures will not be surprised to see these places as like as their homes. Malay tolerance to other cultures is perhaps the unique in the world which makes visitors comfortable in this country.

In conclusion, it can be said that Malaysia is very attractive and a potential region for tourism as it has very suitable weather and good communication system. Together with these, it has highlands, islands, historical places and theme-parks as well. It can attract different kinds of tourists. In terms of economy, every year people keep coming and thus Malaysia gets good economic returns. But besides economy, if we look at the social, cultural or environmental impacts of tourism, it has both positive and negative impacts which may make tourism Malaysia a controversial issue.

Endnotes

1. Klang Valley is a historic-geographical title traditionally used to designate a particular district named Klang District which from the very past is comprised of two *mukims* (sub-district) namely, Klang Town and Kapar Klang Town locating some 32 km south-west of Kuala Lumpur belonging to the Royal Town of the State of Selangor. Klang is one of the principal gateways of Malaysia. From geographical and geological points of views, people now often treat Kuala Lumpur as part of greater Klang valley. In this research, we have used Kuala Lumpur and Klang synonymously to identify greater Kuala Lumpur.
2. Since Kuala Lumpur is much clearly known to the people without any ambiguity, we frequently use Kuala Lumpur in our research, instead of saying Klang valley all the time. Yet, Klang valley and Kuala Lumpur is synonymously used for a similar identification.
3. In regard to local people's perception, two areas named Taman Impian Ehsan, situated near to UPM (University Putra Malaysia) and Taman Midah is located close to Ampang, a very busy commercial zone of Kuala Lumpur. Both these communities belong to broader Klang Valley region within the circumscription of Kuala Lumpur. A total of 200 households taking 100 from each locality are included in the survey to obtain all detailed about their community feelings and people's attitude towards tourism.
4. In tourism literature, the terms 'travel' and 'tour' are often used interchangeably to provide a synonymous meaning which encompasses a temporary movement of a persons from his/her immediate residence and community where he/she stays permanently and thus gets involved on a daily work-environment moving to a place which is different from it (see Chadwick, 1994; Page et al., 2001).

References

Antonakakis, N., Dragouni, M., &Filis, G. (2015). Tourism and growth: The times they are a-changing. *Annals of Tourism Research, 50*, 165-169.

Aronsson, L (2004). The Development of Sustainable Tourism. London: Thomson Learning.

Awang, K. W. (2010). Tourism policy development: The Malaysian experience. *The Arab World Geographer, 13*(2), 150-158.

Backhaus, N. (2005). *Tourism and nature conservation in Malaysian national parks* (Vol. 6). LIT VerlagMünster.

Badri bin Haji Masri (1991): "The growth and prospects of Domestic Tourism" In International Conference on Tourism: Development Trends and Prospects in the 90's. Organized by, Department of Urban and Regional Planning. Faculty of Built Environment. Universiti Teknologi Malaysia, 16 to 18 September, 1991. PP-1-10.

Badaruddin, M. B. Som, M., Puad, A., Jusoh, J., & Kong, Y. W. (2006). Island Tourism In Malaysia The Not So Good News. A paper published by the Department of Building and Planning. Penang: Universiti Sains Malaysia. pp 1212-1219.

Brohman, J. (1996). New directions in tourism for third world development. *Annals of tourism research, 23*(1), 48-70.

Bryden, J. M. (1973): Tourism and Development. Cambridge: Cambridge University Press.

Buckley, R. (Ed.). (2004). *Environmental impacts of ecotourism* (Vol. 2). Cabi.

Buhalis, D., & Costa, C. (Eds.). (2006). *Tourism management dynamics: trends, management and tools*. Routledge.

Buhalis, D., & Laws, E. (Eds.). (2001). *Tourism distribution channels: Practices, issues and transformations*. Cengage Learning EMEA.

Burkart, A.J. and Medlik, S. (1974). Tourism: Past, Present and Future. London: Heinemann.

Burns, P. M., & Novelli, M. (Eds.). (2013). *Tourism and social identities.* London and New York: Routledge.

Butcher, J. (2007). *Ecotourism, NGOs and development: A critical analysis.* London and New York: Routledge.

Butler, R., Hall, C. M., & Jenkins, J. (1997). *Tourism and recreation in rural areas.* John Wiley & Sons Ltd.

Byström, J., & Müller, D. K. (2014). Tourism labor market impacts of national parks: the case of Swedish Lapland. *Zeitschriftfür Wirtschaftsgeographie,58*(2-3), 115-126.

Chadwick, R. (1994). 'Concepts, definitions and measures used in travel and tourism research' in J.R. Brent Ritchie and G. Goeldner (eds). Travel, Tourism and Hospitality Research: A Handbook for Managers and researchers. New York: Wiley. P-65.

Chan, J. K. L. (2015). Responses and green tourism initiatives at a national park in Sabah, Malaysia. *Tourism in the Green Economy*, 146.

Clem Tisdell (2001). "Tourism Economics, the Environment and Development Analysis and Policy": Edward Elgar Publishing, Inc.

Coccossis, H., & Nijkamp, P. (1995). *Sustainable tourism development.* Avebury.

Coles, T., & Timothy, D. J. (Eds.). (2002). *Tourism, diasporas and space.* Routledge.

De Kadt, E. J. (1979). *Tourism--passport to development?: Perspectives on the social and cultural effects of tourism in developing countries* (Vol. 65). A World Bank Research Publication.

Eagles, P. F., McCool, S. F., & Haynes, C. D. (2002). *Sustainable tourism in protected areas: Guidelines for planning and management* (No. 8). IUCN.

Edgell Sr. David L, Allen Del Mastro Maria, smith Ginger, Swanson Jason R. (2008). Tourism policy and planning. Amsterdam: ELSEVIER.

Fennell, D. A. (2008). *Ecotourism: an introduction.* New York: Routledge.

Franklin, A. (2003). *Tourism: an introduction.* London: Sage.

Gao, J., Li, Y., Fu, J., Zhu, Y., & Ding, P. (2015). Environmental impact of sustainable environment policy: A case study from Jiuzhaigou Nature Reserve, China.

Ghosh, R. N., Siddique, M. A. B., & Gabbay, R. (Eds.). (2003). *Tourism and economic development: case studies from the Indian Ocean region*. Ashgate Publishing, Ltd.

Goodwin, H. J. (1998). *Tourism, conservation, and sustainable development: case studies from Asia and Africa* (No. 12). IIED.

Gössling, S., & Hall, C. M. (Eds.). (2006). *Tourism and global environmental change: Ecological, social, economic and political interrelationships* (Vol. 4). Taylor & Francis.

Gutierrez, L.R. (2015). The Environmental Effects of Tourism Architecture on Island Ecosystem in Cayo Guillermo, Cuba. Journal of Environmental Protection, 6(09).

H. Robinson. (1976). A Geography of Tourism. London: Macdonald & Evans. PP-XXI.

Hall, C. M. (2008). *Tourism planning: policies, processes and relationships*. Pearson Education.

Hall, C. M. (ed.). (2007). *Pro-poor Tourism: Who Benefits? Perspectives on Tourism and Poverty Reduction*. Clevedon, Buffalo and Toronto: Channel View Publications.

Hall, C. M., & Lew, A. A. (1998). *Sustainable tourism. A geographical perspective*. Harlow, Essex (UK): Addison Wesley Longman Ltd.

Hall, D. R., & Brown, F. (2006). *Tourism and welfare: Ethics, responsibility and sustained well-being*. CABI.

Hall, D., & Richards, G. (Eds.). (2002). *Tourism and sustainable community development*. Routledge.

Hohl, A. E., & Tisdell, C. A. (1995). Peripheral tourism: development and management. *Annals of Tourism Research*, *22*(3), pp.517-534.

INSAN 1989. Langkawi- From Mashuri to Mahathir: Tourism for Whom? Kuala Lumpur: INSAN The Institute of Social Analysis.

International Conference on Tourism: Development Trends and Prospects in the 90s have; organized by Department of Urban and Regional Planning, Faculty of Built Environment, 1991.

Karim, A.H.M Zehadul and Baker, Mohd. Isa and Chan Hua Chiang (2010). The Living Condition in the Historic City of Penang in Malaysia. *South Asian Anthropologist,* 10 (2) 165-173

Karim, A.H.M Zehadul and Md. Noon, Hazizan and Mohd Noor, Noor Azlan and Mohamad Diah, Nurazzura and Mustari. (2014). Tourism in Malaysia: Problems and Prospects in context to Socio-cultural and Environmental surroundings of the country. *South Asian Anthropologist,* 14 (2), 119-128.

King, V. (2009). Anthropology and tourism in Southeast Asia: Comparative studies, cultural differentiation and agency. *Tourism in Southeast Asia: Challenges and new directions,* 43-68.

Kolas, A. (2008). *Tourism and Tibetan culture in transition: a place called Shangrila.* London and New York: Routledge.

Lea, J. (1988). Tourism and Development in the Third World. London: Routledge.

Leete, Richard (2007). Malaysia: From Kampung to Twin Towers, 50 years of Economic and Social Development. Selangor (Malaysia): Oxford Fajar Sdn. Bhd.

Liaw, J., & Majungki, J. (Eds.). (2001). *Proceedings of the World Ecotourism Conference, the right approach, held at Kota Kinabalu, Sabah on 17-23 October 1999.* Institute for Development Studies (Sabah).

Lis, S. (2009). Impacts of Tourism-An assignment about the development of tourism in Majorca.

Liu, A. (2006). Tourism in rural areas: Kedah, Malaysia. *Tourism management, 27*(5), 878-889.

Lovelock, B. (Ed.). (2007). *Tourism and the consumption of wildlife: Hunting, shooting and sport fishing.* Routledge.

Mason, P. (2010). *Tourism impacts, planning and management.* Routledge.

Mathieson, A., & Wall, G. (1982). *Tourism, economic, physical and social impacts.* London: Longman Scientific and Technical.

Mathieson, A., & Wall, G. (1982). *Tourism, economic, physical and social impacts.* Longman.

Mathieson, A., & Wall, G. (1989). *Tourism, economic, physical and social impacts.* London: Longman Scientific and Technical.

Mbaiwa, J. E. (2005). The socio-cultural impacts of tourism development in the Okavango Delta, Botswana. *Journal of Tourism and Cultural Change, 2*(3), 163-185.

Mieczkowski, Z.T.(1981). Some Notes on Geography of Tourism; A Comment. Canadian geographer.25: pp 186-191.

Müller, D. K., & Jansson, B. (2007). Tourism in Peripheries: Perspectives from the Far North and South. Cambridge (England); Cabi.

Murphy, P.E.(2013). Tourism: A Community Approach. New York AND London: Methuen

Musa, G. (2000). Tourism in Malaysia. *Tourism in South and Southeast Asia*, 144-156.

Nejati, M., Mohamed, B., & Omar, S. I. (2014). Locals' perceptions towards the impacts of tourism and the importance of local engagement: A comparative study of two islands in Malaysia. *Tourism: znanstveno-stručničasopis*, *62*(2), 135-146.

Nor'Ain Othman. (2007). *Tourism Alliances & Networking in Malaysia*. University Publication Centre, Universiti Teknologi MARA.

Orbasli, A. (2002). *Tourists in historic towns: Urban conservation and heritage management*. Taylor & Francis.

Page S J, Brunt P, Busby G and Connell J (2001). Tourism: A Modern Synthesis. London: Thomson Learning.

Phillips, R., & Roberts, S. (Eds.). (2013). *Tourism Planning Community Development-Phillips SOCIETY*. Routledge.

Pye, E. A., & Lin, T. B. (1983). *Tourism in Asia: the economic impact*. Singapore University Press for International Development Research Centre, Ottawa, Canada.

Rátz, T. (2000). Residents' perceptions of the socio-cultural impacts of tourism at Lake Balaton, Hungary. *Tourism and sustainable community development*, 36-47.

Richards, G., & Wilson, J. (Eds.). (2007). *Tourism, creativity and development*. Routledge.

Russel, R.V. (2003). Tourists and Refugees. Annals of Tourism Research, Vol.30, No.4, pp833-846.

Ryan, C. (1991). *Recreational tourism: A social science perspective*. Routledge. Sampson, Charlie 2011 Rural tourism, New Delhi: Discovery Publishing House.

Sathiendrakumar, R., & Tisdell, C. A. (2001). Tourism and the Economic Development of the

Maldives. C Tisdell(ed) (2001). *Tourism economics, the environment and development: analysis and policy*. Edward Elgar Publishing.

Smith, M. K. (2015). Tourism and cultural change. *The Routledge Handbook of Tourism and Sustainability*, 175.

Smith, S. L. (1995). *Tourism analysis: a handbook* (No. Ed. 2). Longman Group Limited.

Smith, V. L., & Eadington, W. R. (Eds.). (1992). *Tourism alternatives: Potentials and problems in the development of tourism.* University of Pennsylvania Press.

Tang, C. F. (2015). Medical Tourism and Its Implication on Malaysia's Economic Growth.

Tang, C. F., & Tan, E. C. (2015). Does tourism effectively stimulate Malaysia's economic growth?. *Tourism Management, 46*, 158-163.

Telfer, D. J., & Sharpley, R. (2007). *Tourism and development in the developing world.* London and New York: Routledge.

Theobald, W. F. (1994). Global Tourism: the Next Decade. Oxford (England): Butterworth-Heinermann Ltd.

Thomson, N. (2011). Moving Towards Tourism. New Delhi: Discovery Publishing House.

Ti, T. C. (Ed.). (1994). *Issues and Challenges in Developing Nature Tourism in Sabah: Proceedings of the Seminar on Nature Tourism as a Tool for Development and Conservation, Held at Kundasang, Sabah on 27-29 March 1994.* Institute for Development Studies.

Timothy, D. J., & Nyaupane, G. P. (Eds.). (2009). *Cultural heritage and tourism in the developing world: a regional perspective.* Routledge.

Tisdell, C. & McKee. (1988). *Tourism Economics, the Environment and Development: Analysis and Policy.* Cheltenham (UK): Edward Elgar Publishing.

Tourism Malaysia. 2014. Tourism Malaysia: Experience Malaysia, Kuala Lumpur: Tourism Malaysia.

Wahab, S., & Pigram, J. J. (1997). Tourism, Development and growth: The challenge of sustainability. London and New York: Routledge.

Yeo Nai Meng. Singapore and Malaysia Tourism: Development, Treats and Prospects in the 1990's, A Paper presented in the international Conference on Tourism Development: Trends and Prospects in 1990's. Kuala Lumpur, Malaysia.

Zillinger, M., (2007). Organizing Tourism Development in Peripheral areas: the case of the Sub-arctic project in Northern Sweden. Müller, D. K., & Jansson, B. (2007). *Tourism in Peripheries: Perspectives from the Far North and South.* pp- 53-69. Cambridge (England); Cabi.

www.ingramcontent.com/pod-product-compliance
Lightning Source LLC
Chambersburg PA
CBHW070600290526
45790CB00002B/739

* 9 7 8 1 4 8 2 8 7 9 9 6 4 *